RICE KEEPERS

By
Rashidah Ismaili

Africa World Press, Inc.

P.O. Box 1892 P.O. Box 48
Trenton, NJ 08607 Asmara, ERITREA

Africa World Press, Inc.

P.O. Box 1892
Trenton, NJ 08607

P.O. Box 48
Asmara, ERITREA

Copyright: © 2006 Rashidah Ismaili

All rights reserved. No part of this publication may be reproduced, stored in a retrieval system or transmitted in any form or by any means electronic, mechanical, photocopying, recording or otherwise without the prior written permission of the publisher.

Cover design by Madonna Davidoff
Book design by Roger Dormann

Library of Congress Cataloging-in-Publication Data

Ismaili, Rashidah.
 Rice keepers / by Rashidah Ismaili.
  p. cm.
  ISBN 1-59221-243-3 -- ISBN 1-59221-244-1 (pbk.)
  1. Rice farmers--Guinea--Drama. 2. Guinea--Drama. 3. Historical drama, American. I. Title.
 PS3559.S56R53 2006
 822'.914--dc22
                    2006000192

Acknowledgements

Rice Keepers is dedicated to those unknown and disremembered names of people, places and times in the lives of African villages, towns, and countries, where resources, human, fauna and flora, have been decapitated and dislocated. These are the histories upon which we the living must honor; stand on the shoulders of those who gave so much and some who did foolish things--all to bring us to a point where we can make life better for Africa and the world. Let us remember Nimba. It is a place where rice grew/grows and whose people were among the first casualties of the Liberian internecine. Let us build a better and healthier world for those who survived.

To my dear friend and teacher, Walter Hadler who ferried me across the painful shoals of imagination and memory. We have worked together these past fifteen years plus, writing, listening re-writing and typing, and talking about content and intent weekly. I am grateful to his wife Georgia for allowing me to take time without any interference, with respect for the work and process. I thank you.

I want to acknowledge the brilliance of my dear sister, Dr. Tuzyline Jita Allan. She has held my feet to the fire with her critique. Over the past year, she has called to ask why and what for this, for that. All of those hours of conversation done out of regard for the work. I am so appreciative.

Finally, I want to say that much of the myth of decapitation, if it is, was something I have heard often. Once, at a conference, I met a woman from New Caledonia. She told me that the French colonials did the same thing. They sought the head of either the chief or main leader and then beheaded him and put it on stakes at the entrance of villages. This is not a condemnation of the French but of the cruelty that some humans have done to others in the course of our sojourn on this planet. It is my prayer that we human beings will accept our responsibility to make positive contributions to this world and leave it a better place when we depart.

May The Ancestors be pleased.

Introduction

Rice Keepers enacts a ritual of remembrance that calls up a moment of ruthless terror visited upon a small rural community in West Africa by the French colonial army in 1940. The eleven-scene drama projects the life-enhancing aspects of women's culture into the traditional theater of colonial power relations in Africa to illustrate simultaneously women's resistance to imperial control and the pervasive impact of colonial trauma. Both themes are held together, with intentional irony, by the image of decapitation, represented in the literal beheading of the major character and the symbolic death of a once-vibrant community. The metaphor also informs understanding of the fractured state of contemporary African life and the protracted crisis of internecine war in the continent. The playwright, Rashidah Ismaili, admits to drawing the inspiration for the play from the cauldron of recent explosive wars in Liberia and Sierra Leone, and the eerie echoes of colonial terror. If there is a gathering sense in Africa that history repeats itself, *Rice Keepers* brings an added incentive to learning from the mistakes of the past by packing vast wisdom into a ritual performance about colonial violence and subaltern resistance.

As ritual drama, *Rice Keepers* illustrates the genre's swaying allegiance to both the symbolic and mimetic realms. Nimba, for example, the site of the dramatic conflict, is both real and symbolic. According to Willi Schulze in *A New Geography of Liberia*, it is "the typical rural town in [Liberia's] hinterland...characterized by its location on a highway or a road junction..., by the presence of various ethnic groups...and by a varying number of traditional and modern administrative, economic, social and cultural functions" (80). Nimba County, of which it is a part, comprises rural and urban towns, as well as "tribal headquarters of paramount or clan chiefs"(80). The towns serve as "functional settlements" used for "accommodating laborers, *training soldiers*, carrying out missionary or educational work, or taking care of sick people...."(81, my italics). Home to large deposits of iron ore, Nimba County is principally a rice-growing district. Other staple foods include cassava and sweet potatoes, but in Liberia and Sierra Leone, rice is the primary food crop. Writing about the Gbandes, an ethnic group located northwest of Nimba, Benjamin C. Dennis, a Liberian-born anthropologist educated in the United States, captures the centrality of rice in Liberia's food culture: "A Ghande may eat bread, potatoes, cassava, plantain, or yams and still consider himself virtually starved for lack of food if he has not had his daily bowl of rice"(34). Dennis sheds important light on the culture-enriching activities of rice production which spread over several phases starting with selecting and clearing the plot of farmland, planting the seeds, weeding the rice fields, harvesting and storing the grain, preparing the rice for cooking, and, finally, cooking and eating the family meal. "The work," Dennis continues, "is well defined with division of labor by sex," excluding only "the very young or old"(23). Female participation in the manual labor is substantial, but in the gendered organization of rice production, women are the rice keepers who give life and provide the essential repair the society needs to function.

While Nimba can be traced to an actual place in Liberia, in *Rice Keepers* it is described ambiguously as "a village in the Guinea Coast"(12) under French colonial rule to highlight its function as a representative site of the colonial encounter in West Africa. Adding to the problem of determining Nimba's identity is the fact that despite Liberia's self-proclaimed independence following the settlement by American freed slaves in 1822, both Britain and France sought to absorb it into their own territories, the latter, according to Russell Warren Howe, being more aggressive in its effort. "From 1912 to 1925," Howe writes, "France kept up frontier pressures in the East; in April 1925, using provoked incidents as a pretext, French forces invaded Liberia and occupied ten villages" (143). By 1940, the year in which the action in the play occurs, with the exception of Liberia and the British colonies of Sierra Leone, Gambia, Ghana, and Nigeria, "the whole of the hump of Africa [was] in French hands" (Buell 901), fueling significant changes in the character of the region. The historian J. D. Page points out that "the French and the British possessed considerable colonial experience prior to the great expansion of empire in Africa"(410). The lessons learned had theoretical and practical implications for the methods devised by both colonial powers to fit the realities on the ground in Africa. Proponents of the British policy of indirect rule, for example, held the view that "if the traditional group life of the native disappear[ed] without a new group life being put in its place, the continent of Africa [would] disintegrate" (Buell 717). Hence they went about "rediscovering or inventing institutions to fit the structure of native administrations, courts, and treasuries"(Iliffe 201), creating a system of surrogate rule thought to be "a typical piece of British indolence"(202). Page describes French colonial occupation of West Africa as "essentially a military enterprise" which legitimated "a centralized and authoritarian system of government with a well-defined chain of command leading down from the Colonial Ministry in Paris, through the Governor-General at Dakar to the governors of the individual colonies, and their provincial commissioners and *commandants de cercle,* the officers in charge of each district"(411). A few Africans employed at the lowest levels of command were drawn from the ranks of chiefs, soldiers, and the educated elite to serve as interpreters and enforcers of colonial mandates. In practice, the line separating these policies was often blurred and, more to the point, from a military perspective, the backlash to insubordination under either system was generally swift and brutal.

Rice Keepers is set against this backdrop in the cold fury of World War II. The women of Nimba are under attack for refusing to grant the local French governor's request for rice to feed the "starving" French army and they are holding their ground against the colonial government's intrusion on their ritual space and its undisguised contempt for their cultural traditions. Earlier in 1908, another governor, G.L.Angoulant, outlining his pacification strategy for the Ivory Coast, affirmed the nexus between France's civilizing mission and military force:

> "Let's face it; at present the native is still hostile to our institutions and indifferent to the efforts we are making to improve his miserable lot. For a long time yet our subjects must be led to progress despite themselves, as some children are educated despite their reluctance to work. We must play the role of strong, strict, parents towards the native, obtaining through authority what persuasion would not gain. The most urgent task is to check every sign of insubordination or ill-will.... The native policy to be followed... must therefore be...benevolent but firm; its firmness will be shown by the suppression of all resistance.... It is desirable to avoid the use of force, but if is used against us we must not be afraid to use it in our turn.... It is essential that bad characters...be isolated and eliminated." (204)

The women targeted for elimination in *Rice Keepers* are neither "bad" nor violence-prone but for an embattled colonial government still smarting from the wounds of World War II, they pose an economic and political threat. First, they are a major source of the cheap labor needed to sustain the colonial economy at home and abroad and, second, their bonding roles as mothers, cultivators of the land, builders of culture and nation constitute a body politic at variance with colonial prerogatives. Like their forebears who took the rice-seed into the New World, the women continue to harness the female crop to achieve cohesion and continuity. The governor's arrogant demand for rice, the most potent symbol of their cultural work, is therefore worth challenging, but in the imperial grammar of power relations, they are seen as "bad characters," who must be "isolated and eliminated." The women's politics, however, is not all local. It has equally grave consequences in the geopolitical theater of war and empire. In *Colonial Conscripts* Myron Echenberg provides startling statistics on the human cost of World War II in French West Africa: "Africans in 1940 constituted almost

9 percent of the French army in France" and "[b]etween the outbreak of hostilities in September 1939 and the fall of France in 1940, some 100,000 men were mobilized in FWA alone." In addition, "[a]t the time of the armistice in June, anywhere from 24,000 to 48,000 Africans were declared missing, of whom perhaps 15,000 to 16,000 became prisoners of war"(88). These figures, coupled with the humiliation and maltreatment of African soldiers on the battlefront, in war camps and in French cities, give added poignancy to the Nimba women's revolt. The nurturing environment of the rice keepers stands in implicit contrast to the chaos of war spilling into their community.

Among the cast of stock characters, two figures best represent the play's clashing perspectives. Hawa, priestess-warrior and custodian of the hearth, believes at once in the protection of the local culture against colonial encroachment and its transmission into the future through participatory ritual. She mediates between the material and symbolic realms, drawing on the power of "these ancient things" (p.29) to empower the people. Elijah, her antagonist, exposes the bitter irony of what is at stake in the elderly woman's struggle for cultural continuity. In his parodic role as conscripted soldier turned collaborator and interpreter, he exhibits the moral confusion inherent in colonial mimicry. As he oscillates between reverence and insult in his response to Hawa's intransigence, he projects the psychic division predictive of surrogate colonial behavior. His energies are suffocated in the end by the double fear of being un-manned by the women and losing face with the colonial authorities. In the ensuing murderous rampage, the spellbinding curses Hawa heaps on Elijah just before her beheading forecast a future of paralysis for the once vibrant community:

> You will suffer for this. No one will share a rice bowl with you. The sounds of this night. The cries of Nimbas will be in your ears until you die…Alone with no one to bring you a cup of water. (*Slaps her hands.*) Your little man will not enter a woman. You will never get a child. You will die alone. (p. 49)

Impotence functions in the play as a metaphor for the loss of self, community and cultural autonomy captured in the culminating experience of dispersal. The trope is also linked subliminally to the image of the barren African woman, whose alienation in life and literature has often been justified in nationalistic terms. Ismaili's depiction of male barrenness, however, puts the anti-female trope into the larger framework of colonial psychology. Elijah's self-consuming desire to enforce a sterile policy results in both individual and collective pain.

The story told in *Rice Keepers* about the African experience of displacement and dispersion resonates throughout postcolonial African literature and film. Ousmane Sembene's *Emitai (God of Thunder)* (1971), for example, exerts a strong influence, as this summary by Frederick Ivor Case makes clear:

In the film, inhabitants of Casmance are faced with the brutality of the French and their African troops kidnapping young men to fight in the Second World War. They are also faced with the colonial administrator's to steal the rice of the community as a contribution to the war effort. It is obvious that the abduction of the young men of the community dramatically alters the importance of the women as they continue to perform their traditional economic tasks, as well as replacing the men who have been taken away. The struggle over rice is a struggle over wealth, and also over a cultural means of expressing fundamental social concepts of appreciation, joy and so on (96).

Ismaili's contribution to the theme of rural women's anticolonial struggle puts a new stress on the all-important function of ritual performance as an idiom of female creativity and political resistance. Through ritual's powerful reinforcing effect, naming becomes a way of remembering and history itself is inscribed as repetition. By stretching the present back into the past, *Rice Keepers* blends history and politics, protest and prophecy, mourning and celebration. Memory frequently breaks into Ismaili's artistic consciousness to illuminate her view of history as recoverable. *Missing in Action and Presumed Dead* (1992), her earliest collection of poems, for example, is accurately described by Charles Sugnet as "a poetry of witness, preserving in its verses the slaves, the activists, the lovers and the political prisoners that the history tries to obliterate." Then there is my recent interview with her which anticipates her concern in *Rice Keepers*. In response to a question about her beginnings, she remarked:

> I was born just at the beginning of the Second World War. Somehow the International World crept into our lives, because many European countries had colonies in Africa, and those colonial subjects were forced to go to the army. My first international connection had something to do with international identity. It had to do with my uncle being taken to go to fight for France. My grandmother couldn't understand why my uncle had to go and defend somebody else's son. Why couldn't that woman's son do a better job? (*Artist and Influence* 1)

The call to remember history and its lessons informs Ismaili's performed activism as poet, dramatist, trained counselor, educator, and political thinker. *Rice Keepers* enriches perforce a formidable tradition.

Tuzyline Jita Allan

Works Cited

Angoulvant, G.L. *La Pacification de la Cote d'Ivoire* (1916). Quoted in *France and West Africa*, ed. J. D. Hargreaves. London: MacMillan and Co. Ltd., 1969.

Buell, Raymond Leslie. *The Native Problem in Africa*, Vol. 1. London: Frank, Cass & Co. Ltd., 1965.

Case, Frederick Ivor. "Ontological discourse in Ousmane Sembene's cinema." In *A Call to Action: The Films of Ousmane Sembene*, ed. Sheila Perry. Westport, Conn.: Greenwood Press, 1996.

Dennis, Benjamin C. *The Gbandes: A People of the Liberian Hinterlands.* Chicago: Nelson-Hall Company, 1972.

Echenberg, Myron. *Colonial Conscripts: The Tiralleurs Senegalais in French West Africa, 1857-1960*. Portsmouth, NH: Heinemann, 1991.

Hatch, James V. et al., eds. *Artist and Influence.* Vol. XIX. New York: Hatch-Billops Collection, Inc., 2000.

Howe, Russell Warren. *Black Africa: From the Colonial Era to Modern Times*. Parts 3 and 4. London: New African Library, 1967.

Iliffe, John. *Africans: The History of a Continent.* London: Cambridge University Press, 1995.

Ismaili, Rashidah. *Missing in Action and Presumed Dead.* Trenton, NJ.: Africa World Press, 1992.

Page, J. D. *A History of Africa.* Fourth Edition. London: Routledge, 2002.

"Rashidah Ismaili Abubakr: Interviewed by Tuzyline Jita Allan." In *Artist and Influence* vol. xix, eds. James V. Hatch, Leo Hamalian, and Judy Blum. New York: Hatch-Billops Collection, Inc., 2000.

Schulze, Willi. *A New Geography of Liberia.* London: Longman, 1973.

CHARACTERS

HAWA: Senior woman (Keeper of the Seeds) — 70s

TUZI: Assistant Keeper of the Seeds — 60s

BINDA: HAWA's sister — 60s

KANDE: HAWA's husband — 70s

KAMARA: BINDA's husband — 60s

FANDIMA: Young woman — late teens, early twenties

MINATA: Young girl — Rice Spirit

TUZI: Becomes **MARY ELIZABETH**

BINDA: Becomes older **MINATA**

ELIJA: Civil servant; 20-65

ZOGBA: A masque that is danced

ACT 1 Scene 1

Nimba, a small village on the Guinea coast; 1940. There are clusters of houses of women who are Keepers of the Seeds. There are huge baskets in a circle in the center of these houses. They are encircled by a fence with many icons adorning.

Mid-afternoon.

KANDE: (*Comes on with fanfare. He stops a few feet away the fence.*)

MINATA: (*Runs on with a stool. She has a raffia cover over her face. Exits.*)

KAMARA: The sky gods are waiting. They ask the earth to open her thighs to receive them. Are you, our mothers, ready to prepare for the rivers?

HAWA: (*Speaks out from her house.*)

Sons of our land, our daughters are ready. They have watched the sky for signs. We wait. We wait.

KANDE: Mother, I must speak with you.

HAWA: Speak then.

KANDE Show your face.

HAWA: (*Comes from forward to the door.*)

MINATA: (*Rushes forward with a stool for her stands behind her.*)

HAWA: Yes, Father, speak.

KANDE: There are places far beyond. A river bigger than our Mlo. The men there are different from us.

HAWA: Why do you speak to me of them? They are not my concern. Soon the time will come when we must prepare the land for sowing. The rains will soak our fields.

KANDE: These men came to me to ask for rice to send to their sons.

HAWA: Where are their mothers?

KANDE: Their mothers are unable to feed them.

HAWA: Have they given shelter to our sons?

KANDE: They are at war and have not farmed during the seasons for planting.

HAWA: We did not make this war. We must spend our time planting and caring for our seeds. If we do not care for our blessings, the gods will be angry and deny us their favor.

KANDE: These men are strong and have guns.

HAWA: Who are they?

KANDE: The Europeans.

HAWA: (*Spits three times.*)

Husband, these are the very ones who came and stole our people.

KANDE: It is so but…

HAWA: Husband, these are the same ones who took our lands. Took the houses of our chiefs and the riches of our families.

KANDE: Yes, Mother, but…

HAWA: Husband, your father, himself, he took the head of one of them. For his bravery, we have created a totem in his honor. Our children sing his praises.

KANDE: Wife, wife, I know. These people are wicked. Yes, they suffer now. But like fleas on a camel, both the camel and the rider get bit.

HAWA:	We have work to do. I must get the seeds from their sacred pots.
MINATA:	(*Walks over to **HAWA** and takes her stool as she stands.*)
KANDE:	Will you share our harvest with the Europeans?
HAWA:	I must speak with my sisters. I will go to them now. (*Walks off.*)
KAMARA:	(*Comes on and goes over to **KANDE**.*) Brother.
KANDE:	Ahhh, Kamara. My wife, ehhhh.
KAMARA:	But what has happened?
KANDE:	Sit, my brother. (*Sighs.*) The Europeans have come to ask for food. Rice!
KAMARA:	But they are rich. They have our gold, and now even as we speak, our men are in their camps working. Have I not told you my son was taken to clear the forest for road? Ah, they are bad. (*Spits three times.*)
HAWA:	(*Comes back.*) Husband, we will share our food if the Europeans will leave our land and return our sons.
KANDE:	Ah-ah, Hawa.
HAWA:	Take them our words. We have no more to say. (*She exits.*)

KAMARA: Brother, I will go with you.

KANDE: Yes, we will go tomorrow. Kamara!

KAMARA: Speak and I obey.

KANDE: We must make a strong offering tonight so that our words will be heard. Hawa is right. The Europeans are wicked.

Lights out.

Lights up.

Court: **HAWA** *is seated on her stool.* **MINATA** *is next to her. The women are arranged according to rank.*

HAWA Nimbas! We must come together now. It is nearing time for planting.

TUZI: Mazoa, last night, I dreamt I saw the first moon shining through the long blades of our fields. I reached up my hand to Her and the rice pods fell off the branches into my palm.

All the women clap in unison three times.

BINDA: My daughter came to me. Her breasts have turned. We will have another mouth to plant our seeds for.

The women clap again.

HAWA: (*Stands, takes a cup from* **MINATA**.)

Mothers of Nimbas and Great Rice Bearer, accept this our prayers for a good harvest.

(*Pours a liquid.*)

Drink, Mother.

(*Pours again.*)

				Drink, Mother.

				(*Pours again.*)

				The women clap in groupings of threes. Spot show bright starlight.

HAWA:			Ahh sisters, the Mother is pleased. We will have a good harvest.

The women clap again.

MINATA:			(*Takes the cup and pours around the rice shoots.*)

A few weeks later.

KANDE:			(*Sitting on a mat eating.*)

				Rice Keeper.

MINATA:			(*Comes forward. She is wearing a yellow print lappa and a head cloth that covers her arms and head. She bows to* **KANDE**.)

KANDE:			Ask your mother to come to me.

HAWA:			(*Appears at the door of her house.*)

				Husband, he who brings water. You have need of me?

KANDE:			Mother, whose hands store the rice. The Europeans have said they must have food. They say they will give us land around Mlo, but our sons are soldiers and they cannot return them to us now.

HAWA:			We have been promised land around Mlo. Inside the homes of Samba and Mende. These are all our lands.

KANDE:			Yes, I have said so. They will give it all back. All.

HAWA:			But where are our sons?

KANDE: In Europe.

HAWA: Hmm, I must speak with the Nimbas.

(*Goes back inside house.*)

KANDE: (*Continues to eat.*)

Minata, I am done. Ah, I cannot eat. The face of the governor. So red with anger. Ahh.

(*Spits.*)

Gods of my fathers and their mothers before them. I have kept your altars. Protect us.

HAWA: (*Comes to the door. Sees* **KANDE** *making offering.*)

Mother, who feeds us, send the rains. We are ready to plant.

There is a loud sound of thunder, then rain. Women's voices raise in praise.

Lights out.

Scene 2

*Curtain rises as drums are heard but not seen. Behind a scrim is a huge dancing figure, a **ZOGBA** with rice seeds woven onto a headdress. On the outside of scrim, fronds line the yard between the houses and the baskets holding rice.*

MINATA: (*Comes on waving blades and dances around each basket. She finishes and puts the rice down on the fronds. Stands near **HAWA**.*)

HAWA: (*Comes on first. She is dressed in ceremonial clothing. A green gown with an elaborate headdress of yellow and green.*)

BINDA: (*Enters on the heels of **HAWA** and rushes to her stool. She puts a rice plant in front of it.*)

TUZI: (*Comes on dancing in sweeping movements.*)

Ho, Mother, Keeper of the Seeds... sit. Sit and wait for the rains.

(*She swirls around. Picks up a small rice plant and touches each of the women and outlines the body of **MINATA**.*)

This our seed waiting for season, make us know that we will be here.

(*Points.*)

Oh Tano, Waters of the Rice Mother, we are coming to you.

(*Dances around.*)

HAWA: Daughters of the soil, I greet you.

BINDA: (*Rushes up and throws rice seeds over her.*)

The fire has been lit and pots boil. Be careful. The guinea fowl is near. She has a nest hidden deep in the forest. She is hungry.

           (*Turns around.*)

           We are hungry. Hmm, look at the fire.

TUZI: (*Ululates.*)

           The Sky gods are speaking. Please, quiet. Listen.

           (*Bends down to the ground.*)

           Ehh.

           (*Body jerks.*)

           Eyah, listen. Ayi! Strange feet.

           (*Screams and falls down.*)

HAWA: (*Stares down at her.*)

           Daughters come. Defend the seeds.

           (*She brandishes a cutlass.*)

           With your bodies. Your very lives.

MINATA: (*Dances around each of the women. Stops near* **HAWA**.)

KAMARA: (*Calls from off stage at first.*)

           Mother! Mother!

           (*On stage now.*)

           There is a hungry child with an empty bowl.

HAWA: Come forward, child. Bring your bowl and eat the food of your land.

TUZI: Stay there. Do not trample the ground. The seeds are trying to see the sun.

KAMARA:	Mazoa, a man has come from the city. He wants to speak with you.
BINDA:	We are preparing for planting. Our bodies will be cleansed tonight. We must not speak with outsiders.
HAWA:	We have time, sister.
	(*She sits on her stool.*)
	Bring him.
KAMARA:	(*Bows and goes off.*)
HAWA:	Where is Fandima?
TUZI:	She is in the rice house.
HAWA:	Tuzi!
TUZI:	Speak, Mother!
HAWA:	Wash her well. Pour extra oil and rice water on her.
TUZI:	She will be a blade lifting its grassy head to the sky with her seeds hidden under pods, housing bowls of our empty hands.
KAMARA:	Mazoa.
	(*Comes on.*)
	Mazoa.
HAWA:	(*Sits holding rice sheaths in her lap and hands.*)
	Speak.
KAMARA:	Mazoa, Europeans in the city have sent this man.
	(*Pulls **ELIJAH**.*)
	Come nearer.

ELIJAH:	(*Enters timidly.*)
	Madame.
HAWA:	(*Nods.*)
TUZI:	(*Mocks him.*)
	Eh-eh, listen. Madame. Eyah, this is your Mother. It is her very hands that tend the rice seeds that brings forth.
ELIJAH:	Mother, I have come from the government.
BINDA:	(*Jumps up.*)
	Which one?
ELIJAH:	M. le...
BINDA:	Zssst! Eh, you mean the frog eater? O Mother, spare him. Spare him.
	(*Walks around him in war like posturing.*)
ELIJAH:	(*Uncomfortable.*)
	Uhmm, the governor has asked me to come here to Nimba to ask you to do your duty. To help feed the sons of France in their hour of need.
HAWA:	Son, have the rains failed France?
ELIJAH:	Mother?
TUZI:	Ah, this one! Is there no rain? Have the gods not granted rain to France to water their soil?
HAWA:	Son, why have you come here? Is your rice bowl empty?
ELIJAH:	No, Mother, but the armies of France are starving. These brave men sit in rain, sun, and snow without bread, water or rice. Their bowls are empty. They ask for food.

HAWA: Son.

(She motions to the women.)

BINDA, TUZI *form a circle around her.* **MINATA** *and* **KAMARA** *stand between* **HAWA** *and* **ELIJAH. MINATA** *holds the cutlass.*

ELIJAH: Mother, it is your custom to feed the hungry.

HAWA: We share the love of the Rice Giver. Our Mother opens her chest and we fill her flattened breasts with seeds. We collect the water from the rains and pour it on her breasts. We share rice with her children. This place France, these men in the City, all, they are not of the soil. They...

ELIJAH: Well, this is overseas France. And all of us—men, black and white—are sons of France.

HAWA: My sons are the children of Nimba. She is the Mother who looked down from the sky and saw people with red hair and swollen bellies. One day, a man went to fetch water because his mother was dying and his sisters were too weak. He filled his jug and started to walk. Then...

(Flicks her hand.)

Ahh, he saw the heads with seeds. Rice. They were hungry. He took them back. Boiled them and fed his mother and sisters.

BINDA *and* **TUZI** *clap in unison three times.*

HAWA: His sister ate and ate, and they fell asleep full and happy. That night the Rice Mother looked down on them and said to the other gods, she wanted to share her breasts so that humans would not be hungry again.

BINDA *and* **TUZI** *clap again.*

MINATA: *(Dances around* **HAWA.***)*

HAWA:	She called the Rain gods and the Sun to witness the suffering. Then as the sun came forward, she blew down the seeds and dropped them on one of the sisters. She awoke and saw them. She called her mother and brother.
MINATA:	(*Dances back and forth between* **HAWA**, **BINDA** *and* **TUZI**.)
HAWA:	The mother told her to pour some of the rice water in a calabash. She washed her face and mouth. She spat out the water on the ground and gave thanks for their lives. The Rice Mother saw this and her heart was moved to tears. The skies opened and the Rain god came down to kiss the women. They planted seeds in the soft earth and always there has been food in Nimba.
MINATA:	(*Dances slowly back around her stool.*)

BINDA *and* **TUZI** *clap again.*

HAWA:	The Rice Mother promised we would always have to eat if we keep our land and feed the hungry.
ELIJAH:	Mother, these men are hungry. Feed them.
TUZI:	But they are not our sons.
BINDA:	They have stolen our sons.
HAWA:	I feed my children. Let the mothers of France feed their sons.
ELIJAH:	There are no rice fields in France.
BINDA:	They are not Rice Eaters.
ELIJAH:	But they are hungry.
TUZI:	They burned our rice fields and now have taken our sons.
ELIJAH:	Forgive them.

HAWA: Tell them to give back our sons. We need them in the fields.

ELIJAH: (*Angered.*)

Listen.

(*Shouts.*)

You must give them rice. It will go bad for you.

HAWA: It is not mine to give. The Rice Mother guides us.

ELIJAH: Are you Christians?

(*Turns to each one.*)

Any of you?

*The **ZOGBA** dances wildly.*

ELIJAH: You heathens! Jesus Christ, the Son of God, says feed the hungry.

BINDA: Tell the mothers of France to pray to their Gods and make their sacrifices so that their sons will be returned.

ELIJAH: You will regret this. The soldiers from the City will come and take your rice. All of it. You will have nothing.

(*Almost begging.*)

HAWA: My Mother, Rice Giver, says let he who comes hungry be fed. Come a stranger. Stay in peace. Leave a friend.

(*Stands.*)

How do you leave?
ELIJAH: Heathens!

(*Gets up.*)

HAWA: (*Brandishes her cutlass.*)

Then let them come. May it be my blood that waters the rice fields.

ELIJAH: Oh God!

(*Runs off.*)

Drums are heard off-stage. **ZOGBA** *dances.* **MINATA** *comes and puts her face on* **HAWA**'*s stomach.*

Lights out.

Lights up a few hours later, early evening.

HAWA *assembles the women for Rice ritual of cleansing. She is the center of a circle.* **BINDA, TUZI** *have chalk on their faces. They enter with fronds in their hands.* **MINATA** *comes on and is placed on a small stool.* **HAWA** *takes a small calabash and pours rice water over her head.*

HAWA: Come frogs and eat the insects that would destroy our rice fields.

Drums continue to be heard off stage. The women dance around **MINATA**. *The* **ZOGBA** *dances off to the right of them.*

Lights dim to out.

Lights up a little later. **KAMARA** *and* **KANDE** *seated upstage right, eating.* **MINATA** *comes on carrying a tray of food. She places a washbowl in the center of the mat. The two men wash their hands and rinse their mouth. Each spit out loudly.* **MINATA** *re-enters and places the same thing on a mat for the women down center stage.*

HAWA: (*Enters and takes her place at the center of the mat. Washes her hands.*)

BINDA *and* **TUZI** *enter. They acknowledge the men and bow on their right knee to* **HAWA**. *They sit and wash their hands. They rinse their mouths and spit loudly.* **MINATA** *comes back on and sits near* **HAWA**.

25

KANDE: (*Eats with his fingers. Pauses mid-way to his mouth.*)

Hawa.

HAWA: (*Looks at him.*)

Yes, husband.

KANDE: The governor made a talk today.

HAWA: The gods are good. They give everyone a mouth. It is up to us to speak. Hah...

KAMARA: Sister, you don't understand. These people are not like us.

BINDA: Husband, the Reverend at the Soul Saving Mission says God made all people the same.

KAMARA: (*Spits three times.*)

Heeh, Binda. Be careful what you say. Have we not always been here? And has not the Rice Mother provided for us? Eyah, do not let her hear you speak of another god. We do not know this god. He is new. Anyway, which kind of god is it that makes everyone the same. The Reverend does not look like us.

TUZI: Yes, Kamara is right. And his wife.

(*She stops eating. Gets up and prances about.*)

Craw-craw. Now laydees, this is a poht. And this is watah. You cannot see them but there are many, many, uhm, things to cause uh di-a-rhea. Running bowels. So you must boil the water. Let it stand, covered—before you drink or cook. Hah! This woman.

(*Spits three times.*)

Oh Rice Giver. Have I not kept our waters clean? Each Thursday I go and take the dead plants, chickens, fish from

	the river. Oh, Tano, who feeds our seeds. I keep you clean.
KANDE:	Ah, listen! Listen to me. Hawa, these people vexed that we don't give them rice. They say we must pay tax.
HAWA:	What is tax?
KAMARA:	A tribute.
HAWA:	We pay tribute to Kande. He is our father. We give goats and rice to the Mission. We give cloth to the schoolteacher. We pay to sell our rice in the market. Ha, too much. We give away too much.
KAMARA:	The white man says all are citizens.
KANDE:	People. Us. We belong to the French State.
BINDA:	How? There are no French here.
KANDE:	Yes, that is so. But they will come. They will come.
HAWA:	(*Sighs.*)
	Husband, hear me. I am the Keeper of the Seeds. As was my grandmother and the mothers of her line. We do not have a girl child to pass on the rice baskets. But Minata and Fandima are our daughters now. Given to us by their own mothers. Tuzi will teach them and keep them after I am gone.
TUZI:	(*Wails.*)
	Ayi, Mother, Mother do not leave me. I am a hopeless foolish woman. I, I...
BINDA:	Tuzi, hush now. Mother is here. See...
HAWA:	Hear me.
	(*Stands on the mat. Stretches her hand back.*)

MINATA:	(*Rushes to her side and gives her a machete.*)
HAWA:	(*Takes the machete. Raises it over her head.*)
	May the Rice Mother give me strength. Husband, if they come here for our rice one must go with me to the grave.
	(*She walks over to the baskets and lays a machete between them.*)
TUZI:	(*Comes forward. Prostrates herself before* **HAWA**.)
	Mother, I will protect the sacred seeds with my very blood.
HAWA:	May you always have to eat.

Everyone claps in unison three times.

Lights dim as everyone slowly exits stage. All in different directions.

Early evening of same day. There is a scrim and people go in front and behind it. **HAWA** *and the women are busy. There is a huge tin tub behind the scrim. A huge* **SANDE** *masque is on a stool near the rice baskets.*

MINATA;	(*Comes on carrying water on her head.*)
VOICE:	(*Off stage.*)
	Hello, good evening.
TUZI:	(*Runs out from upstage left.*)
	Stop! Stop!
ELIJAH:	(*Burst on stage.*)
	Ah! Get out of my way, woman. I have come from the office with a letter from the Ministry of War.
	(*He walks briskly and stops abruptly when he sees the masque.*)

MINATA:	(*Runs on stage and covers the masque with a cloth and stands in front of it, facing* **ELIJAH**.)
TUZI:	(*Hurries back on. Stands in between* **ELIJAH** *and* **MINATA**.)
	You cannot enter here. We are busy. No one can come in.
ELIJAH:	Ah you! Still you are doing these ancient things.
	(*Superior voice.*)
	Old Woman, this is the middle of the twentieth century. Do you know that?
TUZI:	And your father was born before you. And his father before there was a France, England....
ELIJAH:	Look!
	(*Exasperated.*)
	Can you read?
	(*Extends a letter to her.*)
TUZI:	(*Peering at the letter.*)
	The white man's words are not clear to me.
ELIJAH:	Oh, give it to me!
	(*Snatches the letter out of her hands.*)
	It says here, "Citizens of France. I am writing directly to you. To appeal o your loyalty to the tri coloures."
TUZI:	What is loyalty?
ELIJAH:	It is the importance of France to you.
TUZI:	Eh, to France? I am Nimba, Rice Grower.

ELIJAH:	You are a disloyal citizen and I shall report you as such to M. le Ministre of War.
TUZI:	What? Small boy, you report me. Cheeps!
MINATA:	(*Comes forward to meet him. She picks up a machete and points it outward.*)
ELIJAH:	But what is this now? Ah, small girl, just what is it you do?
TUZI:	Our children are prepared to defend to the death our seeds. (*She walks and stands next to MINATA.*) My son, if you are hungry we will feed you. But these men of France, they must ask their mothers for food. They are not Nimba.
ELIJAH:	Well, I am both French and African. And as your son, I ask you to send food to the town. We will send it to France. By boat. (*He starts off. Speaks at first with his back to her.*) If not, they will send troops my mother. France needs the rice. They will not allow their men to starve. (*Turns to her... pleading.*) They will not countenance you saying no to them.
TUZI:	And we Nimbas? What of us? If we share our gifts who will repay us? France, hah!
ELIJAH:	(*Walks sadly off.*) Jesus is my witness. I have warned you.
TUZI:	Eyah, you. (*Calls after him.*)

ELIJAH:	(*Stops turns.*)
	Yes.
TUZI:	When the troops come, will you be with them? Are you loyal?
ELIJAH:	(*Comes to attention.*)
	I am an officer. I shall lead the troops. Yes, I am loyal.
TUZI:	(*Takes a machete from **MINATA**. She touches each basket. Extends it outward to him and then at her neck.*)
	This is our sacred duty to assure our people's lives and to praise our Mother, Rice-Giver. Son…
	(*Walks over to him.*)
	We will defend our rice to the last drop of blood.
	(*Turns her back.*)
	Come a stranger. Stay in Peace. Leave a Friend.
	(*Spins around to him.*)
	Who are you?

Lights out.

*Almost midnight, the same night. When curtain opens the stage is set for ritual cleansing. The sound of feet stomping and hands clapping is heard. Night noises of frogs chirping are loudest. Behind the scrim is a **SANDE**.*

VOICE:	Oh Mother, we come to praise you.
SINGLE VOICE:	Mother of Rice. Giver of the first seeds.

All join in and say: Oh Mother, we come to praise you.

HAWA *enters followed by* **MINATA, TUZI, BINDA** *and* **FANDIMA** *shrouded. They are clapping and stomping on the ground. They stop in front of the* **SANDE**. *They bow and continue towards the rice house.* **HAWA** *sits on her stool.* **MINATA** *stands next to her with the machete.* **TUZI** *and* **BINDA** *go behind the scrim and they come back with a big tin tub. They place the tub in front of* **HAWA**.

HAWA: (*Has a rice plant on her lap. She stands and raises it.*)

Mother, you have given us to eat.

TUZI *and* **BINDA** *clap in unison three times.*

HAWA: We come with joy and love. We come to bathe our daughter.

BINDA: (*Walks over to one of the baskets. There is a stand and on it a jug of water. She brings it to* **HAWA**.)

HAWA: Come, my daughter.

FANDIMA: (*Steps forward.*)

HAWA: And our Mother saw us, her children, pulling berries from trees and flies from the air. Yet our bellies called for more. Our children cried and died too soon. And You saw us Mother and sent us seeds.

(*She raises the jug.*)

This water, this rice water. May it wash all hunger and sickness from your path.

FANDIMA: (*Steps into the tub.*)

BINDA: (*With* **TUZI**, *dip water from a barrel and put it into the tub.*)

HAWA: (*Comes over to the tub. She hands* **MINATA** *the jug and slowly removes* **FANDIMA**'s *shroud.*)

BINDA and **TUZI**: (*Singing.*)

> Our Mother gives us to eat. We are Nimba. Our hands and arms are rice that grows the seeds.

Lights dim.

BINDA *and* **TUZI** go over to **FANDIMA** *and hold her shroud.*

HAWA: (*Pours the rice water down on her.*)

FANDIMA: (*Sits in the tub. We see her bare back.*)

BINDA and **TUZI**: (*Singing.*)

> This your daughter
> comes to you, Mother. Make her like a rice field.
> Give her many seeds.

HAWA: Keep hunger away from your children's door. Let them have food to eat and water to drink. And keep France in France.

MINATA: (*Comes forward and is undressed as is* **FANDIMA**.)

Lights out.

Scene 3

Curtain opens as **KANDE** *and* **KAMARA** *enter. Behind them is a scrim. Women are busy going back and forth, on and off stage.*

HAWA:	(*Walks from Rice House.*)
	Sisters.
TUZI:	(*Rushes on.*)
	Mother.
KANDE:	(*Stands near on the mat.*)
	Hawa!
HAWA:	Husband, we are ready. Tuzi!
TUZI:	Yes, Mother.
HAWA:	Is all ready?
TUZI:	We are ready?
	(*Goes off stage, right. We see her behind the scrim.*)
KAMARA:	(*Comes on stage and sits on the mat with* **KANDE**.)

Heard but not seen, drums and singing. A procession lines up and snakes across the stage. A **SANDE** *masque leads it and is place center stage.* **TUZI** *ululates and waves rice fronds over* **FANDIMA**'s *head. They come to a halt in front of* **HAWA**.

HAWA:	(*Stands.*)
	Oh women of the soil, Keepers of the rice seeds, we have come to bring out our stalk that comes naked, open.

All in unison: Receive her, oh Mother.

MINATA:	(*Moves in a circle around* **FANDIMA**. *She places the machete in front of* **HAWA**. *Stands between* **HAWA** *and* **FANDIMA**.)
HAWA:	And the Rice Mother promised if we humans would clear the land and water her sacred seeds, she would always feed us.

All clap three times.

TUZI:	(*Walks over to* **FANDIMA** *and raises a rice plant over her head.*)

Drums continue off stage. The **SANDE** *masque dances.*

HAWA:	Binda.
BINDA:	(*Comes hurrying.*)
	Hawa, Keeper of the rice baskets.
	(*She bows.*)
	Fandima!
	(*Prostrates herself.*)
	So, even with the armies of France at our door, we continue. May the Rice Mother look down upon us and grant us protection against our enemies. Those who would takeaway our food and leave us hungry.
HAWA:	(*Accepts a calabash of rice water and dips her hand in it. Rinses her mouth and sprays around* **FANDIMA'S** *feet.*)
BINDA:	(*Walks over to the cooking area and fills bowls of rice. She brings one to the men and another to* **HAWA**.)
HAWA:	(*Dips her fingers in the bowl and feeds* **FANDIMA**.)
	Here, eat Rice Keepers.
FANDIMA:	(*Opens her mouth and eats.*)

MINATA:	(*Goes and sits next to* **FANDIMA**.)

All clap in unison three times.

HAWA *goes to each person and feeds them. After everyone is fed, they clap. Finally, she sits as* ***BINDA*** *and* ***TUZI*** *serve the rest of the meal.*

KANDE:	Hawa!
HAWA:	Husband!
KANDE:	That boy came to see me today while you were away.
TUZI:	That Elijah.
HAWA:	What does he want with us? They have taken our very son. Maybe he is wandering alone and hungry. We do not know.
KAMARA:	Ah sister, war is bad-bad. Eyah.
BINDA:	That man, Elijah, he is the mouth of the Governor. Eeh, his poor mother.
HAWA:	We must ask the Mother for guidance. The whites are not like us. They do not wish to hear no from black mouths.
TUZI:	Yes, Mother, you are wise and right.
KAMARA:	We must give them what they want, Hawa. I heard at the market that the army came for food in Nimba. The chief refused. They took him to jail. They say the village must pay 500 francs each day and a kilo of rice as long as he remains there.

As he speaks there is reaction of "Ahhs" and "Cheeps" from all.

TUZI:	(*Walks by* **FANDIMA** *and feeds her as she passes.*)
	I have heard too of jailings and sacking the maize crops from the Cestos. They took from their saltboxes.

HAWA: (*Raises her hand.*)

Enough! I must think. I must think.

VOICE: (*Off stage.*)

A stranger comes hungry and thirsty.

HAWA: Come forward, stranger. Stay in peace. Leave a friend. There is always food for another mouth.

TUZI: Mother, we have not completed our feast.

KANDE: We are not able to see outsiders now.

BINDA: They have not been cleansed.

KAMARA: Evil spirits.

All speak together, over each other.

HAWA: Minata.

MINATA: (*Comes to her.*)

HAWA: Take food to the gate and say to the stranger to come back later.

MINATA: (*Gets the food and goes off stage.*)

FANDIMA: (*Shifts around and begins to eat.*)

BINDA: Nimbas, now that you are entering the sacred time, we must look for a mate.

TUZI: The land is ready for the hoe.

KAMARA: A hand full of seeds is waiting.

BINDA: The calabash is overflowing.

MINATA:	(*Runs back on stage.*)
	Mother!
HAWA:	What is it, Seed of the Land?
MINATA:	It is the one who carries the words of the white man. He refuses our food.
KANDE:	(*Slowly rises and goes off stage.*)
	Let me see who it is.
HAWA:	(*Rises and sprinkles him with rice water.*)
	The seeds are hard and strong. Age is more than passing time.

All clap three times.

KANDE:	(*Goes off stage.*)

Lights dim to out as angry shouts are heard. The **SANDE** *masque is held in a bright spotlight. It dances aggressively.*

Lights out.

Scene 4

Later same night, around 3:00 A.M.

As curtain rises there are bright balls of lights behind scrim. Voices and feet running in the dark are heard.

Lights up slowly.

FEMALE: Eh-eh, what is it?

CHILD: Oh Rice Mother! The fields! The fields!

Lights brighten, stage is orange-colored.

HAWA: (*Comes on hurriedly as she adjusts her lappa.*)

Nimbas! Nimbas!

BINDA, TUZI *and* **FANDIMA** *come over to her.*

HAWA: France has come to take our food!

(*Points.*)

Kete is under fire. We must soon boil water for the rice pot. They will arrive hungry and bleeding. Ahh, war.

(*Turns to them.*)

Go back to sleep. I will sit here and keep watch. The Rice Mother will tell me what to do.

Slowly the people go off stage.

MINATA: (*Comes and sits at* **HAWA**'s *feet with machete in her hands. She puts her head on* **HAWA**'s *knees.*)

HAWA: Sleep, Little Shadow. Sleep.

Lights dim on them as the orange glow upstage shines and smoke rises.

*Next day, early afternoon. Smoke upstage wafts up at intervals. The scrim is lit in silhouette. **SANDE** masque is spotlighted. People in small groups are huddled together. Crying is heard.*

HAWA: (*Comes down stage left from behind the scrim.*)

Oh Rice Mother. What to do? More mouths to feed. Ah, there are so many seeds in a pod.

(*Faces right stage.*)

How, who is it? Come in Peace.

ELIJAH: (*Comes on and stops short.*)

What? Who?

HAWA: These are Kete people. Their fields and homes were torched lastnight.

(*Turns her back to him.*)

Out of thousands only a few remain.

ELIJAH: But what happened?

HAWA: (*Turns to him.*)

What happens when you put a torch to sisal and wood? It burns.

ELIJAH: Was there a fight? Ah, these people. No wonder the white man takes us for fools. We are always fighting each other. Drinking palm wine. Too quick to strike out.

HAWA: How do you know this? There was no clan war. Yes, there was a war but it was not Kete who started it. We saw them. The lorries. All of them with tri-colors. French soldiers. They came and…

ELIJAH: Auntie, I have warned you. I said to all of you the French

	are not going to allow their soldiers to starve. Give them some of the rice and all will be well. But no, you, you…
HAWA:	The Kete do not fight. Everyone knows this. They make clothes. Painted cloth with special colors. Basket makers. They own no lorries. No guns. They live in peace. The other clans protect them.
ELIJAH:	Well, they must have done something.
HAWA:	Yes, they did. They grew small rice. Made their cloths and baskets. As they have always done. It is their own ancestral lands from which they were drive. Unarmed, their village has been sacked and burned.
ELIJAH:	The French are honorable. They do not massa….
HAWA:	Hah! Kete have many villages around here. Traditionally, they are protected because their gods do not allow them to fight. They cannot shed blood.
ELIJAH:	Anybody who does not put the calabash firmly on their head cannot cry when it falls and breaks.
HAWA:	Kete people stay on their own lands. They work hard.
	(*Sighs.*)
	People will not be pleased to hear of this news of the Honorable French.
ELIJAH:	Do not mock them! The French have many guns. They will use them to defeat their enemies.
HAWA:	Why?
ELIJAH:	(*Sputters.*)
	Why, well, uh, no one… No country allows…
HAWA:	Why are they at war now? Which tribe do they seek to conquer?

ELIJAH: Ah, foolish old woman!

HAWA: Yes, you small boy. You call me foolish woman.

ELIJAH: (*Embarrassed.*)

Auntie, I, pardon. But Europe has no tribes or clans.

HAWA: Who do they fight? Why can't they feed their own soldiers?

ELIJAH: Auntie, this war is between, uh…

(*Over explaining.*)

Europeans, French and…

HAWA: Yes, I know that. That is why we want our sons back.

ELIJAH: Uhm, France and Germany, England and… And because we are French, we must defend France.

HAWA: My child listen. I am Nimba. We are all from this Great Mother Africa. France is a place where no rice grows. Where there is war with many lands. It is to this place where cold winds blow and water freezes. Where the sun shines but on white snow. There it is where they have taken our sons. They put on them strange cloths. Do they make cloth in France? Ah, no mind. I am an old foolish woman who cries for her son and the sons of my sisters. I weep for Kete whose looms and trees, cloths and houses are ash. Who will tend the vegetables and flowers now?

(*Turns and points to the scrim.*)

They are without homes of their own. Even here as I speak amongst my own things, French soldiers raise their guns at our heads. Their fingers await, torching our houses. Ahh child, who are these people you call friends?

ELIJAH: (*Moved but defensive.*)

	But, but we are French citizens. We must support the Mother Country.
HAWA:	(*Ululates.*)
	Mother, forgive him. Do not strike this land with your anger.
	(*She turns on him.*)
	Speak what you were sent to say. You are unclean and we have just finished our Rice Keepers ceremony. Say your words and then I will say too.
ELIJAH:	If you believed in Jesus and went to church, you would not fear anything. Me, I go every Sunday to Immaculate for mass. It is a big beautiful cathedral. Just like in Paris. All the French officers and their families go. They...
HAWA:	I do not fear. Now, speak their words. I have people to feed.
ELIJAH:	(*Stands stiff as if at attention.*)
	Two trucks will come in a fortnight to pick up rice. They will return at intervals until the quota is met.
	(*To her as if translating.*)
	Until you have given the required tribute.
HAWA:	Until we starve. We are Nimbas. Everyone knows we are the best rice growers.
	(*Sighs, turns to look at people behind the scrim.*)
	So it is just the Ketes and Nimbas.
	(*Faces him.*)
	Who will be next? The French are not rice growers. Who will tend the fields when we are gone? You? Hah!

ELIJAH: (*Uncomfortable.*)

You have no need to go. They want only a portion of your food. Not all. You will continue to farm.

HAWA: You must go now. I have been in your presence too long. My skin feels as if locust descended on me.

(*Sways.*)

Oh Mother, Rice Giver. We have always obeyed you. We have planted and watered our fields. Saving for the dry season. Ahh, times change.

(*Starts off.*)

I am approaching old age. Soon I will go to join the ancestors. Ah, but what then? Who will cook the rice?

ELIJAH: Auntie, you will see. You are wrong. The French are not like other Europeans. They will not destroy you. Share. They will share.

HAWA: Go now. We have said our words.

ELIJAH: (*Goes towards stage right.*)

They will send trucks in a fortnight. Please Auntie, share with them.

(*He turns and exits.*)

*Lights dim to out as **HAWA** goes back behind scrim.*

Lights out.

A few hours later, people laying mats behind the scrim.

HAWA: (*Enters from the Rice House.*)

Ah, let me sleep now. Mother watch over us. Reveal to me that I might wake in the morning with knowledge.

(*She spreads her mat.*)

Nimbas, I am sleeping now.

Lights dim as people continue to move about behind the scrim. A young man walks on from right stage. He is carrying a basket on his head.

HAWA: (*Dreams, rises from her mat. She stretches her arms towards the young man.*)

Son?

YOUNG MAN: (*Walks on. Stops.*)

Yes, Mother.

VOICE: (*Off stage.*)

I greet you in the name of our Glorious land, France. Citizens, France is suffering. She is under the heels of enemies.

YOUNG MAN: Yes, but who are you?

VOICE: I am a servant of France and come to tell you of the honor I have to inform you of your chance to serve France.

YOUNG MAN: (*Stands still.*)

But I do not know France. I am Nimba. These are my lands. I am the son of Hawa and Kamara... Let me go! Mama!

Lights flash. There is a struggle. The basket falls.

HAWA: (*Wakes up. Reaches out.*)

No! No! Give me back my son.
(*Falls back.*)

Lights out.

Scene 5

Curtain opens with a scrim covering most of the stage. Lights from side give a half-lit view. Several covered people move behind it. **SANDE** *masque dances. A slow dirge on drums is heard.*

FANDIMA: (*Walks on in front of scrim stops.*)

Mama! Mama Hawa! Ayi!

MINATA: (*Comes running on. She carries a small sack around her neck. She stands next to* **FANDIMA**. *Machete drawn.*)

FANDIMA: Hide yourself child. Hide! They have come for our rice. Mama Hawa will not give it to them. She will die instead.

MINATA: I am the Rice Spirit. I will not run. I…

(*Stops, points.*)

Ayi! Ayi!

FANDIMA Oh Rice Mother, look. They are here. They are destroying your fields!

Behind the scrim much movement. Torches are seen, cries are heard. The **SANDE** *masque leaps up and down.*

HAWA: (*Comes rushing forward.*)

Ah daughter, it is as we feared. They have come for our rice. That man, Elijah, is leading them. They have found small pots but are not satisfied.

MINATA: Oh Mama, what to do?

HAWA: You have been trained from birth. You know what to do. I have heard they torture and devour young girls. If they come for you, you must do as you have been taught. The Rice Mother will protect you. Do not lose hope.

Rice Keepers

FANDIMA: We have hidden the seed-rice, Mama.

HAWA: Good.

TUZI: (*Rushes on.*)

Hawa, Rice Keeper!

HAWA: Sister, come near.

TUZI: They have taken Kande and Kamara.

MINATA: Papa!

HAWA: Never fear.

TUZI: I cannot find Binda.

FANDIMA: I saw her in the fields.

HAWA: Fandima, you must take this child and hide yourselves in the bush.

FANDIMA: Mama.

MINATA: Mama…

(*Stands erect.*)

I am the holder of the machete that cuts the bush. If I go, the weeds will overtake the rice plants and Nimbas....

HAWA: No child, you carry the seeds with you. You and Fandima must start new fields away from here. From them… Away from here.

Off stage: Ayi! Ayi!

ELIJAH: Mother! Auntie!

(*Rushes on in uniform.*)

HAWA: (*Stands in front of* **MINATA** *and* **FANDIMA**.)

I am not your mother. My sister could never birth to such a one as you. You, with the blood of our family on your hands.

(*Spits.*)

MINATA *and* **FANDIMA** *back off behind the scrim as* **TUZI** *and* **HAWA** *form a shield.*

MALE VOICE: (*Off stage.*)

Seize the old woman. She is the one. She knows where the rest of the crop is.

ELIJAH: Mama speak! Tell me and you will be spared.

TUZI: Tell you what?

ELIJAH: (*Angry.*)

Where you have hidden the rice.

HAWA: But, you know the way. Our way. We are Nimbas. Rice is our gift. We have shared once, twice.

ELIJAH: That was not enough. You are greedy in time of need of France in her darkest hours. Now we want it all.

HAWA: And for us? Who will grow it? Who will plant and care for it? What is remaining for us?

ELIJAH: We will give each person a sack. Enough for a … a month.

TUZI: You, if we came to your house and said, "Get out. Leave!" And you said. "But where will I go?" And we said, "Well, you can sleep under the trees in the fields." And you say, "But, what of my house, my bed, my clothes?" And we say. "Well, you have your life. But I will give you a cup of water. A bowl of food for a month." Tell me, soldier, what would you do?

BINDA: (*Stumbles on. Her clothes are torn.*)

Ayi! Ayi! Hawa, my husband, your husband. Look!

(*Points off stage.*)

They are hanging from the trees.

(*Points and collapses in* **HAWA's** *arms.*)

HAWA: (*Turns to go.*)

TUZI: You, you have killed your father, uncle.

ELIJAH: No, no it is you! You have caused their deaths. You have angered them. You small-small village people will not stop the French. Hah!

HAWA: (*She encircles him.*)

But we small-small village people have rice and they, the big French Army, have none. Their mothers and fathers do not grow rice. They steal our men. Rape our women, young girls and kill old men.

(*Spits.*)

You, man, hear me.

(*She raises her arms.*)

You will suffer for this. No one will share a rice bowl with you. The sounds of this night, the cries of Nimbas will be in your ears until you die. You will die alone, with no one to bring you a cup of water.

(*Slaps her hands.*)

Your little man will not enter a woman. You will never get a child. You will die alone. I, Hawa, curse you. I Hawa, Rice Keeper put my mouth on you. You will never smile again.

(*Spit three times.*)

***TUZI** and **BINDA** slowly wind around and come stand next to **HAWA**.*

ELIJAH: Hah, foolish old witch. I am a Christian. I pray in the same church as the colonels. You, you cannot save yourself.

(As she speaks, he shields his face and genuflects.)

VOICE: Get her! That one!

*Lights blink. Someone in uniform grabs **HAWA**. We see them struggle. A bayonet is raised.*

Voices are heard: I got it. I got it.

(Lights show movements in slow motions flashing. A head on the tip of a bayonet is seen in silhouette.)

Lights out.

Scene 6

1989: *Curtain opens with military band music under which muted drums are heard. A **SANDE** masque dances grotesquely. Lights dim with a spotlight on a bed upstage left. A body slowly rises.*

FANDIMA: (*Older now. Sits up slowly. Puts feet on the floor. Adjusts her lappa.*)

Mama Hawa, ayi, ayi.

(*Holds her stomach.*)

Mmm, Eya. They came in the night. They sought to steal our rice. But ohhh, Rice Keeper, you, you Hawa, ah. Mama you knew. You knew.

(*Gets up slowly enacts the scene.*)

MINATA, TUZI and **BINDA** *come from right stage. Spotlight follows them. They each carry heavy baskets on their heads. **MINATA** carries the machete. **HAWA** stands alone pointing. Giving instructions. Torches are seen behind the darkened scrim. Piercing screams are heard. One final scream. A moment of silence. Lights flash. The **SANDE** masque dances next to **HAWA**. Lights out for five beats.*

FANDIMA: Ayiiiii!

(*Falls back on bed.*)

Lights raise slowly to full.

MINATA: (*As an adult, rushes on.*)

Mama! Mama! But now, what is it? Ah, these dreams again. They have started, eh.

FANDIMA: Daughter, Spirit of the Rice Mother.

(*Falls on her shoulder.*)

	I saw them. All, Hawa, Binda, Tuzi. I saw them. Kamara too.
MINATA:	Shh, yes, yes. Mama Hawa is with me.

(*She gets up and goes to the altar. Adire cloth covers the basket. She bows before it.*)

Yes, it is time but we have no rice fields here to open. To be watered. The rain falls on cement and on tinned rooftops.

(*Sighs.*)

Ahh, Mother, we are bun-bun left to rot at the bottom of rice pots. No one comes to scrape us out. To eat the sweetness of seeds soaked in palm oil. Ahhh.

FANDIMA But daughter, you have seen them. The young girls who came last night. You heard their stories. Ohh, Rice Mother, who will feed your children? They have run from the fields leaving the seeds without water. The ricebirds will feed on them. There will be nothing but emptiness. Then worms will crawl out from trees. The rice birds will not touch them. Their bellies fill with seeds and they will watch as the worms settle. Eating, eating the stalk. The leaves. Nothing. Nothing will be left.

(*Cries and goes to the altar.*)

Mama Hawa, I am not strong like you. I have tried to live.

(*Watering rice seeds in plastic buckets.*)

Forgive. Forgive!

MINATA: Mama Hawa knows. She will guide us.

FANDIMA: (*Turns to* **MINATA**.)

Daughter, I am getting old. When Mama Hawa was with us. She bathed me as I have bathed you. Now, we have no one.

MINATA: Yes Mama, we will get another. Some new people from up-country have arrived. They were running from fighting between Williams and Kpo.

(*Helps* **FANDIMA** *to bed.*)

Sleep, Mama. We will find a way to carry on.

FANDIMA: The altar, I must bathe it.

MINATA: Sleep, I will do it. Sleep.

FANDIMA: (*Lays back.*)

Just now, I will rest.

MINATA: (*Gets up. Walks over to the altar.*)

Mother, Rice-Giver. I have seen one. A small girl. She is strong. Carried her baby brother on her back for two days. She looked for food for them. Fought a soldier trying to abuse her. Eyah, that one, Mother.

(*Pours rice water over the altar.*)

That one. Save her.

Later that same night, **FANDIMA** *is having a nightmare.*

FANDIMA: (*Sits up in bed. Looks around.*)

Ohhh, they have taken her head. Mazoa! Mazoa! Where? Have you seen it?

(*Covers her head.*)

So many people coming and going. Running. They, they put her head like a coconut on the end of their machete. Carried it around to the villages. To frighten the others. Hawa's head.

(*Cries.*)

And then they took it to France. It is there in a strange house.

(*Sighs.*)

We, we buried the rest of her and a **SANDE** masque. The Rice Mother herself came down from the skies. On the wings of twelve butterflies. She fastened a **SANDE** to her shoulders and took our Hawa with her. Oh Mother, watch over us. So much suffering now. This one, yeke-yeke. And that one yeke-yeke. In the old days we talked. Two wise people sat down to reason things out. Now...

(*Spits.*)

The old ones are dying. Too weak and afraid. No one sits around. The stools have been burned for firewood. We have no rice because we have no money. We have no money because we have no land. Ayi, ayi, ayi, Nimbas!

(*Sinks down.*)

No wonder you have no backs. Your necks are sore. Bent from looking down at your feet. Ahhh, (Falls back on the bed.)

*Lights dim on her. Next morning, **MINATA** comes on stage.*

MINATA: He-eh, this world!

(*Crosses stage and faces the bed.*)

Ma Fandima.

FANDIMA: (*Slowly rises from her bed.*)

Daughter.

MINATA: Ma, I say, you won't know what these two eyes have seen. Eyah!

FANDIMA: A four-legged man and a three-armed woman carrying a two-legged goat.

MINATA: (*Sits*).

That foolish man, Elijah.

FANDIMA: You mean say the man Ma Hawa cursed. The one who burned Nimba?

MINATA: The very one.

FANDIMA: Where?

MINATA: In town. I was going to market when one big motor car came along. I say, it almost knocked me to the ground. Then I stood and looked him in his eyes. Cheeps!

*A **SANDE** dances slowly on stage and moves around the two women. They continue to speak taking no notice of it.*

FANDIMA: Did he know you?

MINATA: No, I think not. But I know him. He rolled his motor car fast-fast. People were knocking over themselves. Trying to get out of his way. But he just went on his way.

FANDIMA: Ah, poor boy. No, poor man. He never changed. Ma Hawa put a curse on him. That man, eh-eh. One man. With his fingers, a pen and a piece of paper could cause people so much harm. Hmm.

MINATA: (*Sighs. Gets up. Unpacks her basket.*)

Ah Mother, you eat?

FANDIMA: Small-small. I ate some soup a little bit ago.

(*Gets up and walks over to the table. Takes a cup of water. Drinks. Goes over to a rice plant growing in the corner and pours the rest of it on the plant.*)

Here, sister, drink.

MINATA: (*Prepares to eat.*)

Mother, I think sometimes about them. About Nimba.

FANDIMA: No daughter. Better not to think.

MINATA: Sometimes I can hear them. The sound of their motor cars. Their feet. Poom! Poom! Poom! Coming closer and closer.

FANDIMA: These are things not to remember. Only speak of them when our daughters go down to the river to be washed.

MINATA: Screams... I hear screams of children and roar of guns.

(*Stops center stage. Circles slowly.*)

It is like the heavens opening. They turn oil on their motors for airplanes and guns.

Each woman carries on their dialogue unmindful of the other. Talking over and cutting off each other.

FANDIMA: Do not think about those times and they will disappear. You will not be able to say it was Monday or Friday. Each day will be the same. Memory...

MINATA: Rice and palaver sauce. Our oil is in France. We who carry poles to knock the palm kernels. We who have pressed and strained oil. Whose reddened hands oil newborn baby heads and mothers swollen breasts. Ahh...

(*Sighs, turns back to her basket and preparations.*)

FANDIMA: Memories are stories we tell to children. To frighten them away from woods and empty fields lest snakes and scorpions get them.

MINATA: (*Sits down and begins to eat.*)

FANDIMA: Ahh...

(*Sits near to* **MINATA**)

We are only humans. What do the gods expect of us?

Lights out.

Later night, early A.M.

FANDIMA: (*Tossing and turning on her bed.*)

Hmmm.

MINATA: (*Sleeping on a mat on the floor. Rouses.*)

Mama! Mama!

FANDIMA: Daughter, please. My stomach is on fire.

MINATA: (*Jumps up. Goes over to table and gets water. Brings it to her in a bowl.*)

Here, Mama, drink.

(*Holds her head up and touches her cheek.*)

You are warm. Fever.

FANDIMA: (*Continues to groan. Finally retches, vomits.*)

Ahh, now. Now I shall be better.

(*Falls back on bed.*)

It is out now. I shall sleep.

MINATA: (*Rushes over with a bucket. Takes a cloth and wipes her face and neck. When* **FANDIMA** *is finished vomiting, she gets more water. Dips her fingers in it and sprinkles* **FANDIMA**'s *face.*)

Yes, Mama, it is out now. Sleep. You will be better in the morning. Sleep.

*Lights dim slowly as **MINATA** takes away the bucket off stage. She comes back on and lays down on her mat.)*

Lights out.

*Next day mid day; darkened stage. **FANDIMA** is propped up on the bed. **MINATA** comes on and goes over to her. Fluffs her pillow.*

MINATA: Ma Fandima, let me get some water for you.

FANDIMA: But tell me, did you see him? Was it Elijah?

MINATA: (*Gets the water and brings it to her.*)

Drink.

(*Sits on the bed.*)

Now, I talked to this young girl. No, woman. I asked her if she was Nimba. She looked like one of the children we took with us when they burned Nimba. She just looked at me.

(*Stops, lost in thought.*)

FANDIMA: (*Hands her the cup.*)

Titie, please.

MINATA: What? Oh yes. Well, Mr. Big Man. Too-too big for we small up country old women. But, I told her to tell him, her boss, to come for supper. I would cook some rice for him. He is a rice eater.

FANDIMA: (*Coughs.*)

MINATA: Ah.

(*Gets up, goes over to the rice plant and pours remaining water on it. Takes the cup and puts it on a table.*)

Well, let me get us something to eat.

(Goes off and on stage as she prepares food.)

FANDIMA: Titie, I was just laying here thinking about her. All these years. We have been driven off our land. Away from our rice fields. Our people have known hunger. We have seen fighting. Guns and torches. Our own soldiers turning their guns on us. We, the Rice-Keepers.... Ahh.

MINATA: *(Stands with a pot in her hands by the table.)*

Ma, do you think it is still around? Somewhere?

FANDIMA: What daughter?

MINATA: Her head. I remember the sound. It is something I shall hear in my ears always. Her song.

> *Nimbas, it is rice we give*
> *to all who hunger.*
> *Use your hands for digging.*
> *Plant slips and seeds deep*
> *deep in the water.*
> *And when strangers come*
> *greet them with a bowl of rice*
> *and a pot of soup.*
> *That is the way of Nimbas.*
> *That is the way of Nimbas.*

And then, whop!

(Grabs her head.)

Ayiiiii!

Lights flash. Lights dim. Torches upstage. A male figure with a machete raised is seen in silhouette. A body is held on the ground. A thud is heard.

Lights out.

Lights up. **MINATA** *and* **FANDIMA** *are eating on* **FANDIMA**'s *bed. There is an off stage knock.*

MINATA:	But what is this?
	(*She goes to the rice plant and pulls out a machete. Walks to the door slowly.*)
	Yes, what is it?
Voice muffled.	
MINATA:	Speak up. I cannot understand you.
MALE VOICE:	It is me.
MINATA:	(*Turns around to FANDIMA.*)
	Ma?
FANDIMA:	(*Waves her hand.*)
MINATA:	(*Opens the door.*)
	Welcome.
ELIJAH:	(*Enters slowly.*)
	Good…
	(*Clears his throat.*)
	Good evening.
MINATA:	(*Closes the door. Stands in front of him with the machete drawn.*)
ELIJAH:	(*Stands still then starts forward. Stops. Bends slowly. Removes his shoes.*)
	Fandima?
MINATA:	(*Backs over to the bed. Places a machete on the floor between them and ELIJAH.*)

FANDIMA:	Daughter, remember, we are Nimbas and a stranger has arrived at our door. Give him to drink and a bowl of rice.
MINATA:	(*Moves off and gets the things.*)
ELIJAH:	(*Turns to look around.*)
	Well, it is smaller than Nimba, but it seems comfortable.
FANDIMA:	The Rice Mother always provides for her children.
MINATA:	(*Brings food and water to him.*)
	Sit.
ELIJAH:	(*Sits on a chair near the bed. He washes his hands in a bowl. Takes food.*)
	May you never thirst. May you never know hunger.

*There is silence as **ELIJAH** eats.*

ELIJAH:	(*Belches.*)
	Oh, sorry.
	(*Embarrassed.*)
FANDIMA:	(*Belches.*)
	Eh now, the air is out. Empty belly full now.
MINATA:	For what are you sorry?
	(*Sighs and gets up. Take his empty bowl. Puts it on the table.*)
FANDIMA:	Yes, I guess you are.
ELIJAH:	(*Makes a big to do over clearing his throat.*)
FANDIMA:	Minata!

MINATA: Mother!

FANDIMA: Give our visitor to drink.

ELIJAH: Visitor? You once called me brother, son.

FANDIMA: That was before.

ELIJAH: Before?

(*Uncomfortable.*)

MINATA: Many years ago.

FANDIMA: When we were all young and you were a soldier for the French.

MINATA: You wore their clothes.

ELIJAH: Uniforms.

MINATA: You carried their guns.

ELIJAH: Weapons.

FANDIMA: You raised your voice to your elders.

MINATA: You laid hands on Mazoa.

ELIJAH: I was a soldier. I did as commanded.

MINATA: You raised your hands against our fathers.

FANDIMA: You pushed us into the forest.

ELIJAH: (*Jumps up.*)

Enough!

(*He shouts. Stands trembling as he stares at the two women. Slowly he begins to pace the room.*)

Please.

FANDIMA:	How you say?
ELIJAH:	(*Continues to moan and pace.*)
MINATA:	We have cried too. We have known empty rice bowls.
ELIJAH:	It was not my fault. I was a soldier. You have to do as commanded!
MINATA:	Look at you. You big and fine. Stomach round. Not like us.

(*Stands, faces him.*)

We have heard our stomach beg for food. Rub front to back with nothing in between. |
| **ELIJAH:** | Please, please.

(*Goes from one to the other.*)

Sorry. I am sorry. |
| **FANDIMA:** | Go to her. Say it to her.

(*Points to the rice plant.*) |
| **ELIJAH:** | (*Involuntarily starts and stops.*)

To her? |
| **MINATA:** | The rice plant. To Mazao. Speak to her. |
| **ELIJAH:** | (*Bristles.*)

What?

(*Steps back.*)

You, you are two crazy women. Living in a past, dead long gone. |

FANDIMA: Yes, away from our land. Here, sitting on concrete. Shut up inside a small flat with no rice fields. No one but us.

(*Cries.*)

No one. They are all dead. Killed.

MINATA: You killed them. You and your friends. If we are crazy, it is you who have made us so.

ELIJAH: (*Implores each of them.*)

I, they were soldiers too. Not my friends. We, we were all soldiers.... Orders.

MINATA: You gave up your rice bowl for blue pants and one gun. They are your family. Tribe. Brothers.

ELIJAH: Mama, please. I am sorry.

(*He is standing in the middle of the room. Slowly walks towards the plant. Clutches his crouch.*)

Mother...

FANDIMA: You must call her louder. She is dead. Buried without her head. We do not know where it is. Call her louder. She has lost her ears.

ELIJAH: Please, it has been so long.

(*Sobs.*)

So long.

MINATA: Yes, it has.

(*She crosses over and picks up the machete.*)

FANDIMA: We are afraid. Afraid and hungry.

ELIJAH: (*Rubbing his crotch.*)

Please, please help me.

MINATA: We begged. We pleaded, Brother, help us. Do not destroy Nimba. We are of the same blood. Save the rice fields.

ELIJAH: (*Turns around from woman to woman.*)

Please.

FANDIMA: (*Struggles to her feet.*)

Tired, I was so tired. I had to carry two little babies. They, they were crying. Mami! Mami! Babaaaah!

(*Screams, sinks back into her chair.*)

ELIJAH: I am not to blame.

MINATA: I tried to get to her. But someone held me back.

(*Reaches forward.*)

Mami! Let me go! Let me go! Mami!

ELIJAH: It was not me. They made me do it. Mama, I could not save my own village. Only my mother and father. We took them to a mission.

FANDIMA: Where are they now? Your own mother and father?

ELIJAH: (*Goes off to right side. Speaks out to audience. Back to them.*)

I saw them off. Set on the road with all their friends. They managed to survive. My mother had never had to walk before. My father was unaccustomed to being so close to strangers.

*Lights dim with shifting spots on **ELIJAH** and **FANDIMA**.*

FANDIMA: Eyah, it was bad-bad.

ELIJAH: I managed to get one of the soldiers to pick them up and drive them to the station. The missionaries were glad to see them. They were scared. So my father became local minister to all the Africans.

(Reaches forth as if to touch someone. Runs his hands down his head and face.)

God, there was so much noise. The guns and the smell of sulfur. Ha, one of the soldiers tried to grab a young girl. She ran through a maze of houses. He banged on one of them and pitched head first into an open seat. It was an out-house.

(Laughs. It is prolonged and becomes a hysterical wail.)

Spot shifts.

FANDIMA: We had to run into the forest. The children were scared. Their little faces and eyes… Eh-wah, the terror. And I too, Rice Mother. Did I not cry to you to help us? To guide us out of the swamps and onto dry land. Yaheeeeee.

Spot shifts.

ELIJAH: I, I did not know what had become of them. I tried to go look that first night… The captain said no one could leave camp because we had a big push the next day. Ayiiiii!

(His hands go back to his crotch.)

The next day was one of the worst days of my life. This useless piece of flesh. She cursed me!

(Softly.)

She cursed me.

(Louder.)

I, I cannot be with a woman anymore.

Spot shifts.

FANDIMA: We walked and walked. The children were crying. Our arms were bent. We could not straighten them. The children slept with their heads on our shoulders. Their breath warmed the cold spots where fear chilled us. And then, we came to Burkah.

Spot shifts.

ELIJAH: It was not my fault. They, they made me do it.

FANDIMA: That night we fell on the mat. I kept seeing her. Ma Hawa. Her body dancing on the ground. Her head on the end of a stick. And those men, they were laughing at her. He.

(*Points.*)

Elijah, he laughed too.

(*Cries.*)

ELIJAH: Sometimes.

(*Circles his face with his hand.*)

Sometimes I think.

(*Beat.*)

When I see a young woman. My mind. I cannot stop it.

MINATA: Where, where did they put it?

ELIJAH: I think first about the spot between two eyes. It is there I think, their thoughts are sitting in a chair. Waiting to be asked to dance.

MINATA: Where is it? We hear her cries but she is ashamed. Without her head how can she greet us?

ELIJAH: Then, I think of a line down from her head to that space. The space above her hair. And, and…

(*He extends his hand as if caressing someone.*)
then. Hamm, The smell of open soil. Oh God! I, I have no release. My hands. With my fingers and mouth. But, my seeds are drying inside me. Rattling in their empty shell.

(*Beat.*)

Please.

MINATA: Mazoa cursed you. You killed her.

(*Beat.*)

Murderer! Murderer!

ELIJAH: (*Holds his ears.*)

No! No! It was not my fault!

FANDIMA: (*Points.*)

Look! Look!

ELIJAH: Nooooo!

(*Faints.*)

Lights dim. A shadow of a headless body dances with the form of a head bobbing in her hand is seen in silhouette.

Lights out.

Scene 7

*There is a scrim and when the curtain rises there are lines of people moving slowly across the stage. In front of the scrim is **FANDIMA** and **MINATA**'s room. They are standing over **ELIJAH**. He is stretched out on the bed.*

ELIJAH: Mmmmmm. (*Groans.*)

FANDIMA: Where is her head?

ELIJAH: (*Struggles to move.*)

Mmmmmm.

MINATA: (*Walks over to the rice plant.*)

Mazoa, you have brought this man into our lives after rock of ages. Is it to *know* where you are?

The light behind the scrim darkens.

ELIJAH: Mmmmm.

FANDIMA: Where? Where is it?

(*Beat, turns her head*),

But what is it?

VOICE: Mama?

MINATA: (*Covers ELIJAH and walks off stage.*)

VOICE: I am so sorry. I...

FANDIMA: But who is it coming in the night to see two old ladies?

MINATA: (*Comes back on with MARY ELIZABETH.*)

Mama, this is the small girl who works with Ee-li-jah.

FANDIMA: (*Draws her near her chair.*)

Come close, child. These eyes fail.

MINATA: (*Pushes her towards FANDIMA.*)

MARY ELIZABETH: (*Slowly goes closer. Stops in front of FANDIMA.*)

Mama.

FANDIMA: Eh! What? Oh.

(*Lights shine*)

Ma Hawa! Mazoa!

(*Falls back.*)

MINATA: (*Walks over to the rice plant. Picks up her machete. Dances around* **FANDIMA** in *the chair and* **MARY ELIZABETH.**)

ELIJAH: (*Moans loud.*)

VOICE: Damn! Damn! Damn!

(*Off stage.*)

ELIJAH: (*Screams.*)

Lights out.

Scene 8

Lights up. **MARY ELIZABETH** *is standing near* **FANDIMA**. **MINATA** *lowers the machete and walks over to bed. Blocks him from view.*

MARY ELIZABETH: I came because you said you were from Nimba.

MINATA: We are Nimba. Rice growers. The keepers of the seeds.

MARY ELIZABETH: My mother was a small child when the expulsion happened.

FANDIMA: How you say?

MARY ELIZABETH: Uhm, when everyone was put out on the road.

FANDIMA: Ah child, that is not the way it was. They came first with guns. Big shots. That was first.

MINATA: Yes, then we saw dust clouds rise. It grew dark. We could no longer see the sun.

FANDIMA: Suddenly, dead silence. We felt the evil crawl over us. No one spoke. Not even a child moved.

MINATA: Ma Hawa pushed me behind her.

FANDIMA: Ma Hawa told me to get the Sande. I went to get it. I...

MINATA: (*Speaks over her. Stands.*)

I took my place. I...

ELIJAH: Hmmm,

(*Sits up.*)

No! No!

FANDIMA:	The air was filled with the loud noise of guns.
MINATA:	The ground shook under me. I nearly fell down.
ELIJAH:	No! No!
	(*Jumps out of bed. He is without his pants. Having a shirt, under shorts, socks. He sees **MARY ELIZABETH** and grabs at his crotch.*)
FANDIMA:	(*Slowly rises.*)
	Something struck me and I fell.
MINATA:	(*Walks away from **ELIJAH**.*)
	Something pulled me and threw me on the ground.
ELIJAH:	Stop! Stop! She's only a child!
	(*Turns blindly around in a circle.*)
	Stop.
FANDIMA:	Fires in the rice field. Run! Run! Ayieeee.
ELIJAH:	Oh my God! No!
	(*Runs to the left. Falls back.*)
MINATA:	I held on to the machete. Mazoa!
MARY ELIZABETH:	But what is it? What…
	There is a five beat silence.
FANDIMA:	(*Walks back to her chair and sits.*)
	Ahhh…

MINATA:	(*Shakes herself. Walks over to **ELIJAH**.*)
	Ah you, where are your pants? You don't see this small girl? Eyah!
ELIJAH:	(*Confused.*)
	But, but…
	(*Slowly walks over to the bed. Picks up covers.*)
	What has happened?
MINATA:	(*Ignores him, goes to **MARY ELIZABETH**.*)
	Come, daughter, sit. I shall make you a cup of tea and some rice.
MARY ELIZABETH:	But, but I am not hungry.
	(*Looks at **ELIJAH** and **FANDIMA**. Sits.*)
	I mean, I ate before. Before coming, I…
FANDIMA:	No mind, child. It is our way. The Nimba way. A bowl of rice and to drink.
	(*Beat. Stares hard at her.*)
	Yes, yes, you are Nimba.
ELIJAH:	My, my pants. Where are my pants?
MINATA:	(*Angrily shouts.*)
	Ah, you small boy. Where is the head of Mazoa? Eh-eh, where? Cheeps.
	(*Preparing food.*)
	Let me get this fire up.

ELIJAH:	Where, where are they? Ah.
	(*Sinks to the floor crying.*)
	Please!
FANDIMA:	(*Covers him with a bed cloth.*)
MINATA:	(*Crosses over with a bowl of rice and a cup of water. Serves* **MARY ELIZABETH**.)
FANDIMA:	May you never know hunger. May you never be thirsty.
ELIJAH:	I don't know. (*Sobbing. Stumbles around.*)
	I, I…
MARY ELIZABETH:	(*Takes the food.*)
	Thank you.
MINATA:	May all be well.
MARY ELIZABETH:	I don't know why I came.
FANDIMA:	It is as it should be.
MARY ELIZABETH:	Since you came.
	(*Pause.*)
	Came to the office. I, I have been troubled.
MINATA:	Come, child, sit and eat.
FANDIMA:	Do not be troubled.
ELIJAH:	(*Moans.*)

VOICE: (*Off stage.*)

Damn! Damn! Damn!

FANDIMA: (*Rises slowly, walks behind* **MARY ELIZABETH** *as she eats.*)

Yes, it is you! Mazoa you have not forsaken us. Still we cannot let you rest in peace. The Rice Mothers and all the Keepers who are with you must be angry with us. That we small people are unable to find your head. Ayi!

MINATA: (*Walks over to them. Gives* **MARY ELIZABETH** *water.*)

Ah, Mama, maybe they ate it. I have heard they are wicked like that.

FANDIMA: (*Sighs, walks to a chair, sits.*)

Ah yes, life carries on in the living.

ELIJAH: (*Tries to get his pants on but is unable to. The legs keep slipping away.*)

Ah, but... but what is it?

FANDIMA: (*Raises her hand and the lights dim.*)

You little man, first you run ahead for your French masters. Barking! Letting everyone know they are coming. Now...

(*She sighs.*)

you run ahead of these hyenas. We have become walking dead. Quick children, hide yourselves.

(*Screams, sinks on her chair.*)

Oh! Oh! The hyenas are ripping bodies apart. Oh, Rice Mother, they will come to you ashamed, with torn arms. It is not the way you made us.

MARY ELIZABETH:	(*Eats slowly.*)
	I try to remember her. I, her face keeps sliding past me. I try to catch her but…
MINATA:	It is our way, to return as we came. To those who send us back to our Rice Mothers, with missing parts, damn, damn, damn!
ELIJAH:	(*At each curse he responds with jerking motions and screams.*)
	Please! Please!
	(*Gets up from the bed. Dances slowly toward **MARY ELIZABETH**. Rubbing his body.*)
	It's dead! It's dead!

Lights out.

*Three days later; **MINATA** and **FANDIMA** are eating.*

MINATA:	Mama, I could not move. I say, Eyah!
FANDIMA:	These people, eh. They have forgotten the old ways.
MINATA:	One of them, he just reached the girl. Pulled her out and took her out of the line. He took her behind the church. She was fighting him but…
FANDIMA:	Hyenas are deaf. The Rice Mother has blocked their ears.
MINATA:	When I heard that poor girl scream.
FANDIMA:	Mazoa, save her!
MINATA:	She just said, Toyibo! Toyibo! Toyibo!
VOICES:	(*Screams.*)

FANDIMA: This rice is sweet, daughter.

MINATA: Yes, Ma Fandima, I could not go out. The soldiers have made a curfew. They say they will shoot anyone outside their doors.

FANDIMA: So…

MINATA: The soldier who took that poor child behind the church. He came out all bloody. His face, ah! Just yelling and yelling.

FANDIMA: Damn! Damn! Damn!

MINATA: The girl ran away.

FANDIMA: May your seeds dry up on the vines and rattle in the winds.

MINATA: He fell down on the ground, rolling over and over. Holding his little man. When one of the army people looked, it was gone.

VOICES: (*Screams off stage.*)

FANDIMA: Hmmmm, Mazoa!

MINATA: They were angry.

(*Becomes agitated.*)

They started shooting. Killing! Ah, Rice Mother; we have turned the guns on ourselves!

(*Sinks to the floor in a moan.*)

Lights out.

Scene 9

Two weeks later, late afternoon. Lights up slowly on same room.

FANDIMA: (*Rises slowly from bed. Gets up. Walks slowly to window. Back-crosses stage to table. Takes a cloth and washes her face, arms, legs, sighs. Goes to rice plant and pours water on it. Goes back to table, gets a bowl of rice. Brings it over to her chair, sits.*)

Lights dim. Scrim behind her opens. There is a red carpet on floor. Four people wearing European masques. One has a face of Mme. Pompadour. There is a palatial guard, a page and well-dressed gentleman. There are two glass cases on the wall. The guard is a guide who does most of the talking. The three stand in front of the cases and strike poses. Their face masques contradict their attire. Each is dressed stylishly.

GUARD: And here Madames et Messieurs we have our trophy cases.

MADAME: (*With a lorgnette, goes closer to case. Backs away.*)

Ah!

GUARD: The heads you see here are those of savages from the darkest Africa.

GENTLEMAN: Hah!

(*Disbelief.*)

GUARD: And now...

(*With flourish.*)

how this came to be. Well, it started in the Pacific. When we were transporting slaves for the cane fields. At New Caledonia, same thing. Big, black, bushy haired buggers. One of the men grabbed a cutlass and sliced a big black one. All the others stopped.

(*Snaps his fingers.*)

That was it. Seems they've got this superstition about being disfigured.

(*Burst into laughter.*)

Them, disfigured.

(*Bows to* **MADAME.**)

Pardon the language.

MADAME: (*Bows.*)

GENTLEMAN: (*Bows.*)

But…

PAGE: (*Bows.*)

Yes, but…

GUARD: (*Holds up hand.*)

Yes, yes, I know. Well, there they were in this outpost of hell. These bastards, ahem, pardon. These blacks, devils. They refused to pay their war tax. Mind you, this the premier rice- growing area of the province. So, the Third Battalion went to collect it. There she was, this female giant. Bones coming out of her noise. Ostrich feathers in her hair.

(*Dances around in grotesque movements*).

She refused the rice.

(*Claps.*)

All the males are hung.

(*Claps.*)

Hoopla! Then she grabbed a machete. Killed about ten and wounded more before we brought her down. But…

(*Twirls.*)

brought her down we did.

(*Stands with hand on his chest…*)

They all imitate his position. Hold pose, five beats.

GUARD: They had this black scout. Brought him forward. While she was knocked down, he chopped off her head. And…

(*Flourish.*)

here she is. Hawa, the Great. Great? Hah-hah.

*They all laugh hysterically. Suddenly lights flash. Head of **HAWA** flies up and above their heads. All the other heads move up and down with clamour. **MADAME**, **PAGE**, **GENTLEMAN** and **GUARD** stand watching the head float upwards over their heads. LA MARSEILLALSE plays as the head ascends. Drums drown out the song.*

Lights out.

Scene 10

FANDIMA: (*On her bed. Slowly jerks awake.*)

VOICE: (*Off stage.*)

Mama! Mama! Please! Please!

FANDIMA: (*Rises slowly. Goes toward the door. Stops briefly in front of the rice plant.*)

Ayi, Mother, what now? Can't a poor old woman rest these days?

(*Walks over to door.*)

No, no. There is no peace when your home has been burned. When your fields cry like women whose breasts swell and burst with milk for a child who lies dead in their arms. Ahh.

ELIJAH: (*Burst into the room as **FANDIMA** opens, the door. Falls at her feet.*)

Mama! Mama!

VOICE: (*Off stage.*)

Damn! Damn! Damn!

ELIJAH: Please! Please!

FANDIMA: (*Stands still three beats, looks down at his head.*)

What is this?

ELIJAH: (*Struggles to his feet pulling himself up by her dress.*)

P-please, Ma Fandima. Help me. Lift the curse. Please!

(*Sinks down on his knees.*)

My God!

FANDIMA:	(*Pulls her dress away and walks to the rice plant. She stands and faces them, points*)
	Ohh, it was you. Your own hands that struck her. You took off her head.
ELIJAH:	(*Moans, almost unable to speak.*)
	Please! Please!
FANDIMA:	For your masters! You showed them you were brave. Hah!
ELIJAH:	Ma! Ma! Ma Fandima!
FANDIMA:	(*Whirls around and gives him her back.*)
	Ahh, you are only a man. Poor thing, what can you do? You are not a rice planter.
ELIJAH:	(*Gets up slowly. Crawls cowering toward her, holding his crotch.*)
	Please, it can do nothing. I cannot dig a hole in which to plant my seeds.
	(*Bends over.*)
	I will die and carry with me my dried, dead seeds. They rattle when the wind blows them. My two buds flapping in the wind. Ahh…
	(*Whirls around and around*)

Lights dim. A silhouette of a shrunken head comes down from the ceiling.

FANDIMA:	(*Swoons as she sinks down near the rice plant.*)
	Mazoa!
ELIJAH:	(*Unfolds reaches up, hands out-stretched. Falls back down again in a heap*).

Lights out, ten beats.

*Lights up. The head is suspended over the bed. On the bed the forms of **ELIJAH** and **FANDIMA**.*

ELIJAH: Mazoa!

FANDIMA: Louder!

ELIJAH: Mazoa! Mazoa!

Lights out.

Later, same day.

***MINATA** walks on in dim light as **FANDIMA** rises from the bed.*

FANDIMA: (*Gets up and walks over to **MINATA**.*)

MINATA: (*Loaded with a heavy basket. Sets it on the floor.*)

Mama, eh! I tire. This my back!

(*Stretches.*)

And these arms, I thought they would give out on me. But …

(*Walks over to **FANDIMA**, bows*)

No, there is still the strength of Mazoa in these hands.

(*Holds out her hand, cries.*)

Ahh, the fields, the fields!

FANDIMA: You must not cry. Save the water for the dry seasons to feed the rice seeds.

MINATA: Mama, there is no more rice. The fields are choking with blood. The soldiers are walking down the little heads as soon as they send shoots up. Just killing and cutting.

	(*Retches.*)
	What will they eat after the rains?
FANDIMA:	Do not fear child.
	(*Takes her in her arms and draws her to a chair.*)
	Shh!
MINATA:	Ma, I had some palm butter and two big fishes.
	(*Cries.*)
	They took them. A soldier jump out the bush. Had a big gun. He asked me for money.
VOICE:	(*Off stage.*)
	Money! Give me your money, old woman!
MINATA:	I said, Son, I am a poor old thing. I have no money.
MAN:	Yes, yes, you do. All old women carry money. Dig in your bosoms and bring it.
MINATA:	I bared my breasts to him. Son, I have no money and I have no milk.
MAN:	Foolish old witch.
	(*A loud crash is heard.*)
MINATA:	Ayi…
	(*Swoons at **FANDIMA**'s feet*)
	He struck me one cuff.
	(*Struggles to get up.*)

I, I fell and, and…

(*Turns around in a circle, confused.*)

I was wet when I touched my head.

FANDIMA: (*Touches her head. Leads her to a chair. Walks over to the table and pours water in a basin. As she prepares a bandage,* **MINATA** *continues talking.*)

MINATA: One small boy came by. He gave me some water. Then, his older sister passed by. She washed my face and gave me a little bowl of rice pap. It is that which got me here. Ayi! Ayi! Nimba, look at me bloody and left to bake in the sun like a dead leaf from a tree. Drop wherever it falls. Oh Mazoa…

(*Crying.*)

I, the holder of the sacred machete. I have been faithful to you. Even as I repeated the words of those missionaries. I called your name. Now, now… Ahh.

FANDIMA: But it is the Mother who brings forth and the father who fells trees for a bed. It is we who hear and see water and blood mix. Who cut cords and carry them to fields. We who know the names of all your mothers and fathers who are here.

MINATA: (*Sits still as* **FANDIMA** *binds her head.*)

FANDIMA: Daughter, the Mother is near.

MINATA: How you say?

FANDIMA: (*Sighs and sits.*)

Eyah, she came to me in a dream. Let us watch and wait.

MINATA: Yes, we will do so.

(*Sighs.*)

I feel better. Let me prepare our meal.

(*Gets up slowly, reels, steadies herself.*)

Yes, yes.

FANDIMA: But where did those come from?

MINATA: As I passed one of the fish stalls, a kind woman said, "Here's to eat mother." And I took this fish. It was bigger than the one the soldier boy took from me.

FANDIMA: Ah, Rice Mother!

MINATA: Thanks and blessings.

(*Unwraps food.*)

And here is rice. Our bin was nearing the bottom.

(*Walks over to a shelf and takes a glass jar and pours rice.*)

May we never be hungry.

(*Turns to the door.*)

MARY ELIZABETH: (*Enters.*)

Mother, I have come.

(*She is carrying a bundle tied in bright cloth.*)

May you never be hungry.

(*She steps inside and she is dressed in traditional dress with a gelee.*)

FANDIMA: Stay in peace.

	(Stands in front of her, smiles.)
	Leave a friend.
MINATA:	*(Stops putting things away briefly.)*
	Stay in peace, daughter.
MARY ELIZABETH:	Mama,
	(Brings bundle to her.)
	Mama, Elijah came to our house last night. He asked my uncle for me. To marry him.
MINATA:	But what is this?
FANDIMA:	*(Walks over to the rice plant.)*
	I saw her. Her head came down and sat right down on the rice plant. She said…
VOICE:	*(Female voice off-stage.)*
	Mba imakoto. Mba imako. Mba imadoto.
MARY ELIZABETH:	*(Turns to **MINATA** and starts toward her.)*
	But Auntie, what…
MINATA:	It is nothing, Titie.
FANDIMA:	*(Walks over to her chair. Raises her hand.)*
	Knock on the door.
MARY ELIZABETH:	*(Goes to the door. Looks at **MINATA**.)*

Come a stranger.

(*Opens it.*)

Stay in peace, oh-oh!

ELIJAH: (*Stands wearing a white boubou.*) I come in peace.

MINATA: Come in stranger, in peace.

ELIJAH: (*Walks in, slips out of his shoes. Brings a small basket to MINATA.*)

May you never know hunger.

MINATA: (*Takes it.*)

Oh, palm butter, bonga, okro and rice… Ah, may you never know hunger.

ELIJAH: (*Walks over to FANDIMA.*)

Mama, last night, for the first time, I slept without the sound of dried shekeres on trees in dry seasons. And when I woke this morning, I felt new. My…

(*Lifts his boubou to her.*)

little man stirred, small-small.

FANDIMA: Bring me her head and I will remove the curse. I will say the words.

ELIJAH: Mama, I asked for her. Oh Mama, in my head, my heart and my stomach there is a bright fire. It burns and burns. Water cannot quench it. Release me, Mama.

FANDIMA: Bring me her head.

MINATA and **MARY ELIZABETH** *continue to talk and put away things. A silhouette of a head is seen behind them and a scrim.*

*Lights encircle **ELIJAH**, **MINATA**, **FANDIMA** and **MARY ELIZABETH**. We do not see the rest of the stage. (Each speaks out facing audience. Sometimes they talk over the other.)*

*Lights on **ELIJAH**.*

ELIJAH: I, I came to her stumbling. I…

MINATA: The ground of a new field is often hard to plow.

MARY ELIZABETH: I opened my clothes to him.

FANDIMA: Yes, it is the way, Little Mother.

MINATA: The field may fight at first.

ELIJAH: I do not understand what happened. I am after all a grown man. And yet, it was as if for the first time.

MARY ELIZABETH: I lay my cloth on the ground.

FANDIMA: That is it, Little Mother. You will be called Hawa.

MINATA: Rice Mother, guide us. Give us a good season.

MARY ELIZABETH: I lay on top the cloth Ma Fandima gave me.

ELIJAH: It has been so very long since I felt the urging.

MARY ELIZABETH: I took my hands and opened myself.

MINATA: She is a good child.

FANDIMA: (*Faces **MARY ELIZABETH** in a diagonal. Extends arms.*)

Yes, rice field. Open yourself wide.

ELIJAH:	I pulled at my clothes like a… (*Beat.*)
	lion. I was a man again.
MARY ELIZABETH:	He fell on me.
MINATA:	Rice Mother send rain to wet the field and make earth soft for planting.
ELIJAH:	I, I could not stop my trembling. I felt my seeds swell inside. Oh, oh, the pain.
MARY ELIZABETH:	He tried to plow but often fell onto a rut.
MINATA:	Open child. Open and breathe.
ELIJAH:	I was a novice. A mere boy. Unable to control myself. I… (*Beat.*) I remember I slipped. Ayi…
MINATA:	Hold on child. (*Turns to **MARY ELIZABETH**.*)
FANDIMA:	Steady!
MARY ELIZABETH:	I guided him and held the plow.
ELIJAH:	And then that child. That woman/child held me in her arms. Me. This tired old man. Hungry and empty for all these years. Oh god! God hear my prayer.
FANDIMA:	Yes, daughter. Oh Mazoa, You are indeed a good mother. You will come for me now…. Soon.

MINATA: (*Turns aside, facing audience.*)
Ma Fandima thinks I don't understand. She plans to go. To leave me here. Alone.

MARY ELIZABETH: I felt rain pour down and legs were wet.

(*Runs her hands over her body. Sighs.*)

ELIJAH: Oh God, I do repent all my sins.

(*Inhales.*)

Thank You.

FANDIMA: Mazoa, it is done. I will wash her with my own hands. Minata will tend the field until harvest. I am soon ready. Eyah.

(*Walks slowly around **MARY ELIZABETH**.*)

Yes, little Hawa, you will bring forth a good harvest.

ELIJAH: (*Turns to **FANDIMA**.*)

Ma Fandima, I must leave now.

(*Walks over to **MARY ELIZABETH**.*)

I will come to you tonight.

MINATA: (*Circles around **ELIJAH**.*)

You promised us. We have kept our word. The head.

ELIJAH: (*Stops short. Stares at her.*)

I...

FANDIMA: (*Goes towards her bed.*)

Eyah.

(*Grabs her ears.*)

Ohh, Ma Hawa. I cannot bear your crying.

(*Turns to* **ELIJAH**.)

You small boy, bring her head this night. I am tired. I must rest. She calls me all day, all night. She is tired of circling about this world. She must have her head so she can go and join the ancestors.

(*Sits on the bed.*)

Go bring it. Bring her head. Tonight!

ELIJAH: I, I must go now. Oh God help me!

(*Rushes out.*)

A loud drumbeat is heard. The **ZOGBA** dances around **MARY ELIZABETH**.

Lights out.

Later, the same day.

FANDIMA: (*Sitting in her chair. Rises with difficulty.*)

ELIJAH: (*Sits opposite her.*)

Here, Ma Fandima.

(*Pushes some papers toward her.*)

Just sign here.

(*Edges his chair closer.*)

FANDIMA: Ah, still you do. You are the same as a boy. Acting like a big man.

ELIJAH: Mama please, that was a long time past. Try not to remember.

FANDIMA: To lose memory is to wander without a path. When you see the moon, you follow it blindly. A star appears and you turn about. Then comes dawn and with the moon at your back and the sun in your face, which way to go.

ELIJAH: This is neither sun nor moon. Just some papers that give you a little place outside the city. A bit of land to raise chickens and you can sit in your yard at night and swat mosquitoes. Hah-ha.

(*Laughs.*)

FANDIMA: And so… Well, well.

(*Takes the papers.*)

Eyah!

ELIJAH: (*Takes them and turns the papers around.*)

Like so.

FANDIMA: Oh well, it looks better the other way.

ELIJAH: (*Getting annoyed.*)

Here is a pencil. You must make a mark and I will fix my name next to it. That makes it legal for you to move from here.

FANDIMA: That means the soldiers will not ask for money and knock my poor Minata.

ELIJAH: Yes, that is what it means. I will see to it that you pass safely. No one will harm you.

FANDIMA: You will do this for me? For us?

ELIJAH: Yes. Oh Mama, you gave me a great gift.

FANDIMA: Ah, you mean your little toy? Hah.

ELIJAH: (*Uncomfortable.*)

Please, Mama. I must return to my office. I have an important meeting this afternoon. We are trying to settle the refugee problems and…

FANDIMA: (*Waves her hand.*)

Let us all go back to our villages and towns. We don't belong here. Our fields are waiting. Our altars and gods have not been watered and fed. They are all angry with us because we have turned our backs on them.

(*Rises slowly and walks toward her rice plant.*)

ELIJAH: Please, Ma Fandima, I am a Christian. Do not speak about your heathen spirits.

FANDIMA: It was those spirits who protected your mothers and fathers and their mothers and fathers… all those times before.

(*Stops and faces him as she speaks. Turns and gets water and waters the plant as she continues to speak.*)

But you. You have grown away from your people.

(*Stops. Standing by the plant.*)

You have no place to go. You are a refugee too. Just like Minata and me.

ELIJAH: (*Angrily jumps up.*)

You old fool! I have plenty places to stay. I am free to go as I choose. I am trying to help you. Now make your mark so I can leave.

Drumming softly heard.

FANDIMA: (*Sighs.*)

Yes, yes, you are right. I am an old fool. And you are free.

(*She slowly crosses over to him. Signs the papers. Hands them to him.*)

Now, bring me her head and I will take it when we go.

ELIJAH: (*Snatches the paper.*)

Mama, I have told you. I know nothing. There was a war. I was a young soldier. The only African officer in a French man's army.

ZOGBA dancer appears up-stage. Drumming continues softly.

FANDIMA: (*Faces him.*)

Her head, bring it. She cries in the night to me. I can get no rest because she cannot enter the ancestor's house without her head. Her head!

(*Voice rises over **ELIJAH**.*)

ELIJAH: (*Grabs her.*)

I, I had to show myself brave.

FANDIMA: Her head!

ELJAH: She defied me. Laughed at my uniform. In front of them the French soldiers, with their cold blue eyes.

(*Shakes her.*)

I had to take control of the situation. Any good soldier must do this.

FANDIMA: (*Breaks free of him. Sways, steadies herself. Walks toward the plant. The machete is on the altar above it. She stops.*)

Mazoa! Mazoa!

ELIJAH: (*Rushes over to her.*)

You understand? I had to do something. It was her fault.

ZOGBA comes forward dancing behind ELIJAH.

ELIJAH: (*Whirls about. His back to her. Hands on his ears.*)

No! No! Not again.

(*Grabs his crotch.*)

Just a while longer. She is warm. Ohh, her strong legs around me.

(*Falls on his knees.*)

Please! Please!

FANDIMA: Her head!

ELIJAH: Oh God! I don't know where it is. They took it. Some of

	the men. Souvenir. Perhaps they buried it. Maybe they took it to Paris. I don't know. I swear I don't know!
FANDIMA:	She came to me at the last full moon.
	(*Looks at the* **ZOGBA**.)
ELIJAH:	Please, she came to me on the full moon and opened herself to me. I filled her with my seeds. Bursting rice seeds. Ohh, do not take this brief joy from me. All these years I have walked, carrying my dried stick around. In my head…
FANDIMA:	Her head!
ELIJAH:	(*Walks trance-like to her.*)
	My head! In my head. I remembered what it was like before. I had nothing but memories and dreams. And then she came to me.
FANDIMA:	Oh, Rice Mother!
ELIJAH:	(*Takes* **FANDIMA** *around the neck and chokes her. He is unaware of what he is doing.*)
	Not now…
	(*Pulls* **FANDIMA** *across the floor.*)
FANDIMA:	Yes, Ma Hawa. This is what we have come to! Our sons become our death. But he is Nimba and, and…
ELIJAH:	Shh, old woman. Stop talking.
	(*Continues to choke her.*)
FANDIMA:	But his seeds. They are planted in her.
	(*Pants in between words.*)
	Ma Hawa.

ELIJAH: (*Drags her body and lets it fall on her bed.*)

Listen, I will take her to the court house and marry her. We shall have some children. I am not too old.

(*Rubs his crotch.*)

I can still cover her well.

(*Almost masturbatory.*)

Mama, God, release the seeds.

(*Looks down on the bed and sees* **FANDIMA**.)

Mama!

(*Tries to rouse her.*)

Ma, Ma Fandima.

(*Staggers back.*)

Mama! Mama!

Drums are louder. **ZOGBA** *dances around* **FANDIMA**. **ELIJAH** *breaks away and runs off stage.*

Lights out.

Scene 11

MINATA: (*Enters, talking over her shoulder, carrying a basket.*)

But what is this? Ma Fandima, I told you. This is a wicked place. Do not leave the door open. I thought I locked it. Mama?

(*Puts things on table. Walks over to the bed.*)

Ha, sleep.

MARY ELIZABETH: (*Off stage.*)

Mama, I see Elijah's car.

(*Walks on carrying things.*)

Quickly, he should be here any moment.

(*Starts toward the bed.*)

Oh, Ma Hawa sleeps.

MINATA: (*Goes to the rice plant.*)

You see, she called your name.

MARY ELIZABETH: Oh, that's strange. I mean, Ma Fandima.

(*Goes to her and tries to straighten her body.*)

Mama, Mama, are you all right?

MINATA: (*Goes back to the table.*)

She sleeps a lot these days. Says she practicing so when she leaves. I won't…

MARY ELIZABETH:	Ma Minnie, come. Come see her. She…
MINATA:	(*Walks across*)
	What's all the fuss?
	(*Takes **FANDIMA**'s hand.*)
	Mama!
	(***FANDIMA**'s hand drops.*)
	Oh.
ELIJAH:	May I enter?
	(*He comes in carrying the papers. He sees them at **FANDIMA**'s side.*)
	What is it?
MINATA:	(*Crying*)
	Ayii, Ma Fandima, ayi!
ELIJAH:	(*Shocked, he now realizes what he has done.*)
	But, but…
MINATA:	The door was unlocked.
	Each person speaks over the other.
MARY ELIZABETH:	But how?
ELIJAH:	But, I, I came to get her to sign these papers.
MINATA:	I told her many times. This is not Nimba of old.

ELIJAH:	I asked her to forgive me. To keep away the curse. She…
MARY ELIZABETH:	(*Sits on the bed, cries.*)
	Ah, poor old woman. Driven from your home. Now…
ELIJAH:	I told her she could have a little house and land with chickens.
MARY ELIZABETH:	She wanted to plant rice seeds again. Nimba has the sweetest rice.
MINATA:	(*Crying.*)
	I should have stayed home. Not gone to the market.
ELIJAH:	(*Walks around **MARY ELIZABETH**.*)
	She signed the papers. I gave her a little house just outside town. Off the road.
	(*Extends his hand with the papers.*)
MINATA:	Ah now, what to do? There is no one left but me. Oh Ma, I do not know what to do. How to do?
ELIJAH:	What to do now? I, I…
MARY ELIZABETH:	Mama, let me help you.
MINATA:	We must wash her. Go, get some rice water in that jar. There.
	(*Points to a jar near the rice plant.*)
ELIJAH:	Here are the papers. You can go away from here now.
	(*Dazed. Trying to show them to **MINATA** and **MARY ELIZABETH**.*)

SANDE masques dances in front and back of **MARY ELIZABETH**.

MINATA: You have been chosen daughter. You are Hawa.

(*She dips her hands in the bowl and begins to wash FANDIMA's face. After she is finishes she goes over to the table and puts the bowl down.*)

Oh.

MARY ELIZABETH: It will not end, Mama. He, he held me and I felt his maleness stirring against my flesh. At first I was afraid and wanted to turn back. But Ma Fandima said I must. She said Ma Hawa had chosen me to be the new Mazoa. So I let him enter my fields and took from him the seeds of life. I…

MINATA: Child, child.

(*Sobs.*)

See, the rice pot is empty. Someone has come and eaten all. Look.

ELIJAH: (*Walks around in a small circle talking to himself.*)

I open my arms. My heart sang with joy. My head was filled with sight and smell of her. Look, look what I give you.

(*Extends the papers again.*)

MINATA: You, Big Man. Come help us. We must take Ma Fandima back to Nimba to bury her.

ELIJAH: (*Stumbles to* **MARY ELIZABETH**.)

Come, I only want to feel your warm breath on my face, my hands on your skin. Ah.

**MARY
ELIZABETH:** (*Backs away from him. Steps on the handle of the machete.*)

Oh.

(*Turns to **MINATA**.*)

Ma Minnie, look. I have it.

ELIJAH: (*Turns his back to them. Starts toward the door.*)

I must go and prepare my bed for her.

(*He reaches the chair by the table.*)

I gave them the papers. She signed. I will come back for you. My dearest. I am going now to prepare for you. I…

MINATA: (*Walks behind him. She blocks his path.*)

**MARY
ELIZABETH:** (*Picks up the machete and walks toward **ELIJAH**.*)

*Lights begin to flicker. **ZOGBA** dances out and around **ELIJAH**.*

Lights out.

Two days later. There are baskets and boxes stacked around the room.

MINATA: Are you sure the car will come?

**MARY
ELIZABETH:** (*Now wearing a boubah.*)

Yes, Ma Minnie. He is my cousin. He is coming in his truck. We can put everything in it. Do not worry.

MINATA: (*Takes the rice plant and puts it by the door. She leans the machete next to it.*)

Ah!

MARY
ELIZABETH: (*Crosses the room and off stage.*)

Ma Minnie.

(*Comes back on.*)

He is here. I will carry out these things first.

(*Picks up a suitcase and goes off.*)

MINATA: Hmm, we going, Ma Fandima. We got the papers. We going to plant the rice seeds for next seasons.

MARY
ELIZABETH: (*Re-enters.*)

I will push theses baskets to the door and my cousin will take them.

(*She pushes them by the exit. Looks about*)

What more to do?

MINATA: (*Rises with a sigh.*)

Nothing. We must leave these things here. When we reach the new house I will make us a bed of straw until we get a new one.

Lights begin to dim as the last box and basket are pushed by the exit.

MINATA: Go along, child. I am coming just now.

(*She turns and goes to the bed.*)

I have the rice plant and seeds for a new harvest.

MARY
ELIZABETH: (*Comes back on.*)

	Ma Minnie, come. We are waiting. We want to reach before dark.
MINATA:	Just now, I am coming. Go along now.
MARY ELIZABETH:	(*Exits.*)
MINATA:	(*Walks around the table.*)
	Damn! Damn! Damn!
	(*She takes a match.*)

Lights dim, as **MINATA** *sets fire to the room.*

Lights out.